THE SUPERNATURAL

The Supernatural

*Making Room
for the
Power of God*

A.B. Simpson

CHRISTIAN PUBLICATIONS
CAMP HILL, PENNSYLVANIA

Christian Publications
3825 Hartzdale Drive, Camp Hill, PA 17011

Faithful, biblical publishing since 1883

ISBN: 0-87509-565-8
LOC Catalog Card Number: 94-71704
© 1994 by Christian Publications
All rights reserved
Printed in the United States of America

94 95 96 97 98   5 4 3 2 1

Unless otherwise indicated, Scripture taken from the HOLY BIBLE: NEW INTERNATIONAL VERSION®. © 1973, 1978, 1984 by the International Bible Society. Used by permission of Zondervan Publishing House. All rights reserved.

Contents

Introduction: The Present Truth 1
1 *The Supernatural God* 5
2 *The Supernatural Book* 17
3 *The Supernatural Life* 33
4 *The Supernatural Church* 45
5 *The Supernatural Body* 57
6 *The Supernatural Hope* 75
7 *The Supernatural Work* 97
Index 107

INTRODUCTION

The Present Truth

> *So I will always remind you of these things, even though you know them and are firmly established in the truth you now have. (2 Peter 1:12)*

While all inspired truth is necessary and important yet there are certain truths which God emphasizes at certain times. He is ever speaking to the age and generation, and He never speaks at random but always to the point and to the times.

When the thought of the age was being drawn to the supremacy of one man and taught to recognize the Sovereign Pontiff as the viceroy of heaven and the direct representative of Christ on earth, God raised up John Calvin to emphasize the doctrine of God's sovereignty and to teach the age that He alone had a right to dominate the hearts of men.

When Formalism had spread its soporific influence over the heart of Christendom, God raised up the Wesleys, George Whitefield, Fletcher and the evangelical leaders of that generation to teach the necessity of the new birth and to emphasize the work of the Holy Spirit.

Later an evangelical movement brought into clear and bold relief the doctrine of justification by faith and the premillennial coming of Christ as against the nominal church teachings of the times.

A generation ago God used the ministry of Charles Finney and the testimony of his followers to bring into prominence the doctrine of a deeper Christian life as an antidote to the worldliness and compromising spirit of the times.

And so from age to age God speaks the special message most needed, so that there is always some portion of divine truth which might properly be called *present truth*, God's message to the times. God is always wanting messengers that understand Him and that preach the preaching He bids, and when He can find such instruments He will always use them and bless their ministry.

There is one line of truth which seems to be preeminently present truth and that is the truth about the *supernatural*.

Man has become so much in love with man that he is in danger of overlooking God. The boasted progress of our times has so dazzled us with its secondary light that we cannot see the glorious Sun that is shining in the firmament of God's heaven. The devil is trying to get the supernatural out of the Bible, out of the church and out of our individual Christian lives. He wants to reduce religion to a human science, obliterating everything that cannot be explained on a rational principle and from natural causes, so that even our blessed hope of the coming kingdom is laughed down and man thinks himself all-sufficient to achieve his own destinies and bring about the highest development of the race.

Over against this stands God's revelation of the supernatural. Let us look at it until it dwarfs our human pride into its true insignificance and give us adequate views of ourselves and our times in the light of the infinite God "from whom . . . and . . . through whom all things came" (1 Corinthians 8:6).

CHAPTER 1

The Supernatural God

In the beginning God created the heavens and the earth. (Genesis 1:1)

The first sentence in the Bible brings us face to face not with men, not even with nature, but with God—"In the beginning God." True, there is a verb "created" that follows; but long before we reach that there is an emphatic pause, and the infinite deity stands before us filling immensity and enfolding within His own being the whole creation and the myriad beings that are afterwards to come forth from His almighty hand. The Bible begins with God, and it would be a good thing if every book and every chapter in every life had the same safe and sublime beginning.

The Bible also ends with God. We turn to the last message and we read in the Apocalypse, "I am the Alpha and the Omega, the First and the Last, the Beginning and the End" (Revelation 22:13). He that began as Alpha is ending as Omega, and between these two extremes lies the whole story of redemption.

If we turn to the last verse of the Apocalypse, leaving out the benediction, we find that the Bible ends with Jesus Christ. It begins with God and ends with Jesus Christ—and between these two divine names lies the whole story of revelation.

In beautiful similarity the apostle's great draft upon the bank of heaven, "And my God will meet all your needs according to his glorious riches in Christ Jesus" (Philippians 4:19), begins with "My God" and ends with "Christ Jesus," while between lies all our need and its infinite supply. What a safe and blessed place to be!

In accordance with this majestic beginning God is always projecting His personality and presence upon the scene of the story of revelation and redemption. There is a sublime egotism in the Bible; that which in others would be unbecoming is in Him absolutely right. Over and over again He asserts Himself, and every instinct of our being recognizes His preeminence, His sovereignty and His right to be supreme. It contains just what man needs to know and recognize, the presence and the glory of his God. It shows what our lives need above all other needs, to know Him, to realize His presence and to live under the shadow of the Almighty.

We sometimes meet men who impress us not so much with their own personality as with the presence of God which they carry with them.

This was the characteristic of Enoch. The only thing remarkable said about him was that he walked in the divine Presence. We read of Samuel and Elijah that each was recognized as "the man of God."

This is what we want in our lives, to know God, to walk with God, to be men and women of God and then to minister God to other men and women.

Whenever God called men into a closer relation or sent them on some higher commission, the call was always accompanied with some marked revelation of Himself.

We find Him coming to Abraham at the crisis of his life as *El Shaddai* and then commanding Abraham to rise to a higher place in conformity to the new revelation that He had given.

"I am God Almighty [*El Shaddai*]; walk before me and be blameless" (Genesis 17:1). I am the Almighty, the Absolute, the Infinite, the All-sufficient God. Now live up to the vision you have had, the revelation I have given. Stand straight up to the standard God has given. Live as if you had a God that is all-sufficient.

God told Abraham, "You have not been living thus. You have not been walking before Me. You have been walking before Sarah, before Hagar, before circumstances, before your difficulties and limitations and infirmities. Now lift your vision above all these, look at Me alone and see in Me the God who is enough, and stand upright in uncompromising faith."

And so henceforth Abraham "did not waver through unbelief regarding the promise of God, but was strengthened in his faith and gave glory to God, being fully persuaded that God had power to do what he had promised" (Romans 4:20-21).

The secret of Abraham's faith was his realization of the supernatural God. And so in describing him in the fourth chapter of Romans the apostle says that he measured up to God, "in whom he believed—the God who . . . calls things that are not as though they were" (Romans 4:17).

When God came to Moses to send him forth on his stupendous undertaking, the only thing He sought to impress upon his mind was the supernatural Presence that was to go with him. His one answer to all the fears and doubts of Moses was, "I AM WHO I AM" (Exodus 3:14). He just drew a great check upon Himself and signed it, leaving a blank line for Moses to fill in anything he pleased. He seemed to say, "I am courage in your difficulties; I am power in your weakness; I am victory over Pharaoh; I am sovereignty over the Red Sea; I am bread for the wilderness and water from the rock; I am the guide for the desert and the conqueror for the Midianites and the Canaanites; I am mercy and forgiveness for the gainsaying people that you lead." And oh, that Moses had also added one thing more, "I am grace and strength to keep even you from missing the Promised Land."

And when Moses still parleyed and procrastinated, God answered with that one final word, "I will be with you" (3:12). Later in the story of the wilderness we find Moses falling back on this great promise and crying, "If your Presence does not go with us, do not send us up from here" (33:15), and the answer came, "I will do the very thing you have asked" (33:17). It was God and God alone that made Moses what he was and Israel what it became.

A New Leader, the Same Presence

This was all the equipment of Joshua for his victorious succession to Moses. "Be strong and courageous. Do not be terrified; do not be discouraged, for the LORD your God will be with you wherever you go" (Joshua 1:9) was the divine assurance. "I will be with you; I will never leave you nor forsake you" (1:5). When a little later Joshua was in danger of looming up too large in his own leadership, God met him and laid him in the dust and took command Himself of Israel's victorious armies of faith. Going forth to reconnoiter the ramparts of Jericho he met a man with a drawn sword, and, true to his soldierly instinct, he challenged him and cried, "Are you for us or for our enemies?" (5:13). The answer that came laid him prostrate on his face. " 'Neither,' he replied, 'but as commander of the army of the LORD I have now come. . . . Take off your sandals, for the place where you are standing is holy' " (5:14-15). I am the Leader and you have but to do My bidding and let Me triumph through you.

It was the vision of God that called Isaiah to his ministry and strengthened him to bear the rejection of his countrymen and to stand alone with God in the midst of a gainsaying people.

Something out of Nothing

There is nothing finer in the Scriptures than His majestic promise to Jeremiah: "This is what the LORD says, he who made the earth, the LORD who formed it and established it—the LORD is his name: 'Call to me and I will answer you and tell you great and unsearchable things you do not know' " (Jeremiah 33:2-3).

This is a very glorious and inspiring promise but the most glorious part of it is the preface and the name by which God introduces Himself to the prophet: "Thus saith the LORD [Jehovah], the maker thereof" (33:2, KJV)—not the Creator of the universe but the Creator of the thing which Jeremiah is about to ask for. It is something which does not now exist and for which the very materials do not yet appear. It is something which, naturally speaking, is impossible. It is something which God has to cut, not out of whole cloth, but out of no cloth. It is something which must be created in order to become a reality and of which He says, "I am the maker thereof; I will create it at the call of your faith; I will form it and then I will establish it."

This is the faith of which the apostle speaks in the epistle to the Hebrews: "By faith we understand that the universe was formed at God's command, so that what is seen was not made out of what was visible" (11:3). That is to say, it is a faith that believes in the unseen and in the creation of things that are not yet real. It is a faith that can take Him for a gentleness you do not have in your temper, for courage when you are like a trembling reed shaken of the wind, for a steadfast will when you are as irresolute as the drifting sand, for righteousness and holiness when every instinct of your nature and every tendency of your training leads you in the downward road, for health and strength when your body is a wreck and the very elements of health are gone, for souls that seem as hard as adamant, and for service where every door appears to be closed and every effort vain. This is the God with whom we are dealing, the God of the supernatural, "the maker thereof . . . Jehovah is His name." Let us recognize Him. Let us trust Him; let us use Him in His infinite all-sufficiency.

"My Spirit Remains"

In the book of Haggai there is a beautiful collection of promises in which God tells His struggling little flock, as they are seeking to accomplish the great work of the restoration in troublesome times and with feeble resources, that His presence is with them: "My Spirit remains among you. Do not fear" (2:5). He says this so they may be strong and work with the confidence of success. In this beautiful paragraph it is striking to notice how often the prophet repeats the lofty name. "This is what the LORD Almighty says" (1:2). It is as though God were ever bidding His trembling children to look up in His face to reassure themselves that He was speaking, that He was there and that He was equal to even this emergency.

It is paralleled by that beautiful promise of Christ to Paul in the midst of his infirmities. "He said to me," or to better translate the Greek, "He *kept saying* to me, 'My grace is sufficient for you' " (2 Corinthians 12:9). Over and over again He repeats to us the assurance of His presence and His all-sufficiency.

When Christ was about to give the commission to His apostles to go forth and evangelize the nations, He emphasized to them that mighty assurance of His Almightiness and Omnipresence. "All authority in heaven and on earth has been given to me.... And surely I am with you always, to the very end of the age" (Matthew 28:18, 20).

This is the warrant for our missionary enterprise, for our boldest faith, for our loftiest endeavor, for our most difficult undertaking. We have the supernatural Christ to lead us as we go forth against principalities and powers and the forces of earth and hell.

We Must Recognize His Supremacy

The reason God emphasizes His supremacy is because of man's ignorant and foolish pride. We live in an age of human self-sufficiency when boasting man is saying, "Come, let us build ourselves a city, with a tower that reaches to the heavens" (Genesis 11:4), and God is saying in divine pity and scorn, "Come, let us go down and confuse their language" (11:7).

But it is not in the spirit of our petty egotism that God is ever asserting Himself. It is because His sovereignty is as necessary for the universe as for His own glory. As He repeats the personal pronoun and stands before us in sublime self-consciousness we feel that what would be presumption in any man is right in the case of God, and that it is essential to the order and well-being of the universe that He should be recognized as All in all.

His sovereignty and supremacy are the supply of all our need. The more we become less and let Him become greater (John 3:30) the more our happiness and blessing will increase. Our own self-importance is the greatest hindrance to the revelation of God in our hearts and lives. In order that He may come in, self must go out. The more we die to ourselves the more room we have to receive Him in His fullness.

There is much wholesome instruction in the incident of the lad whose father was reprimanding him because of his poor progress in his studies. The little fellow was complaining that he did his best and that he was not able to remember the things he read. The father had noticed in the boy's room a good many yellow-covered books, and he said, "Charlie, I want you to empty out that basket of apples, on the sideboard."

Charlie emptied out the apples, and then his father said, "Go out to the carpenter shop next door and bring me a basketful of chips and shavings." He did as he was told and when the basket came back it was half full of chips. "Now," said his father, "put in the apples." Charlie put in a few of the apples and they began to tumble off.

"Put them in," said his father, "put them all in."

"I can't," said Charlie, "they won't go."

"Why won't they go?" asked his father.

"Why," said Charlie, "because the basket is half full of chips and it won't hold all the apples now."

"Ah," said his father, "that is the trouble with you. You have been trying to fill your head with wholesome knowledge when it is already crammed with foolish story books."

Carry the story a little higher and we will find the secret of our spiritual failures. We have been trying to fill with the Holy Spirit hearts that are already filled with a thousand things. We have been trying to make Christ King while all the time the old rebel self was in His way and usurping His throne.

A Foretaste of the Future

Finally, the revelation of God in our hearts and lives is but the overlapping of that glorious revealing of God for which the age is waiting. We are looking for "the blessed hope—the glorious appearing of our great God and Savior, Jesus Christ" (Titus 2:13), and He comes first in the inner vision and then in the outward revelation.

He is projecting His personality upon the heart of His waiting Bride. He is making Himself intensely real to those who will let Him, and for them some day He will burst through the veil of sense and they will cry as they behold Him, "Surely this is our God; we trusted in him" (Isaiah 25:9).

In the old days of New England a company of our Pilgrim fathers was in great destitution, waiting for a ship from England with supplies which was long overdue. One good woman in the company had been praying in strong faith and telling the people that the ship would come in due time. Sure enough, one evening they looked out over Boston Bay and the ship was in full view and their hearts were filled with joy and hope. But when the morning dawned the ship had disappeared. Some of them said it was a mirage, or perhaps a refraction of the coming ship projected by indirect rays of light before the ship itself came into full view, but they felt sure that as they had seen the vision they would surely see the ship. And they did. Before the week was over she was docked in the harbor and was dealing out her stores of bread to the starving colonists.

And so God gives us first the vision of the living, personal, glorious Christ and soon our eyes will see Him and we will be with Him forever. Let us understand Him in all His glory and some day "we shall be like him, for we shall see him as he is" (1 John 3:2).

CHAPTER 2

The Supernatural Book

For you have been born again, not of perishable seed, but of imperishable, through the living and enduring word of God. For,

> *"All men are like grass,*
> *and all their glory is like the flowers*
> *of the field;*
> *the grass withers and the flowers fall,*
> *but the word of the Lord stands forever."*
> *(1 Peter 1:23-25)*

There is no testimony that needs to be more emphatically pressed upon the hearts of men today than the inspiration and supreme authority of the Word of God. The malignity of Satan and the pride of human culture are striving as never before to eliminate the supernatural from the Holy Scriptures and change the Book of God into a mere collection of ancient writings, saved out of the wreck of the world's literature.

The Bible stands apart from all other books, and has survived and will survive all the attacks of its enemies. It is like the electric torch that shines over the water of New York Harbor, struck by the wing of many a seabird that dashes against it in its reckless flight, but still shining on unmoved while the foolish and reckless assailant falls bleeding and wounded at its feet.

It is an anvil which has worn out many a hammer of hostile criticism, while the anvil still remains unshaken amid the wreck of all that have assailed it.

It stands above all other books in a supreme and sublime isolation. "Bring me the Book," said Sir Walter Scott to his son-in-law, when he was dying. As Lockhart asked him, "What book, Sir Walter," his simple answer was, "There is but one—the Bible."

When Alexander Duff was on his voyage to India with a large quantity of excellent baggage, including a splendid library of more than 800 volumes, the ship on which he was sailing was wrecked off the Cape of Good Hope, and when the rescued passengers reached the shore the only thing of all his baggage that was saved was a Bible that the waves had washed upon the sands. As he picked it up and removed the wrapping he found it was perfectly uninjured, and he was so deeply touched with the incident that he opened it and read some of its precious promises to the little company that stood around him on the shore. All his splendid books had perished, but the Bible remained as the only salvage from the wreck. To him it was a beautiful figure of that which afterward became the object of his life, that the Bible was the only book that would remain out of the world's literature, and the only book which was worth giving to India, the land for which he was going forth to live and die.

The Bible Survives

All the literature of the ages must perish in the flight of time, but, like Duff's rescued Bible, God's Word will live and survive the wreck of ages, and also give to those that embraced it an immortality as glorious as its own.

It is very sad and humbling to see the tendency among so many of those who ought to be the defenders and the teachers of this holy volume to win a little cheap popularity and wear the reputation of higher culture by joining in the ranks of those who, if they do not reject it altogether, will compromise its supremacy and question its infallible authority.

The Bible is either everything or nothing. Like a chain which depends upon its weakest link, if God's Word is not absolutely and completely true, it is too weak a cable to fix our anchorage and guarantee our eternal peace. Thank God, we have reason to accept it as the supernatural revelation of the supernatural God, the word not of man, but the Word of God that lives and abides forever.

It has survived the assaults of its critics as the

ages have gone by. And while not claiming to teach philosophy and science, yet even philosophy and science with all their progress have not been able to establish a single argument against its credibility. While the so-called science of one generation has challenged it, the advanced knowledge of the next generation has but confirmed it.

The time was when the first chapter of Genesis was supposed to contradict the established facts of science by teaching that light was created in the beginning, while the sun and the other heavenly bodies were not created until the fourth day. But a few years later God led science to discover the spectroscope, and with it the fact that light did exist before the sun, and that Moses was in perfect accord with the real facts of nature.

Reverent scholarship is finding out every day that even in the very allusions of God's Word to the sublime facts of nature there are hidden harmonies with the great truths which science is only now discovering, and when Job spoke of the sweet influence of the Pleiades and David sang in the 19th Psalm of the light speaking, they were really teaching some of the deepest facts and latest discoveries of the majestic sciences of optics and astronomy. Out of every conflict this divine Book will come forth vindicated and victorious.

> Like some tall cliff that lifts
> its awful form,
> Swells from the vale and midway

> leaves the storm,
> Though round its breast the rolling
> clouds are spread,
> Eternal sunshine settles
> on its head.

Let it suffice to bring five witnesses to the supernatural character and supreme authority of the Word of God.

1. Miracles

This Book appeals to us by a supernatural test. It claims as its credentials the superhuman power of its witnesses. It appeals to the infinite Creator to certify to its message by the works which are known to be beyond the power of any created agent. The stock objection to miracles which has become famous through the writings of David Hume is that a miracle is contrary to the uniformity of nature and therefore cannot be true, because we are bound to believe the uniform testimony of nature against any single testimony that seems to contradict it. This argument is absolutely as weak and foolish as our experience of nature is limited and partial.

An explorer told a chief from the Upper Congo about the ice of our northern climates, and assured him that he had seen rivers completely frozen over and water become as solid as stone. "Such a thing is contrary to all the experience of nature," replied the chief, and he laughed him to scorn. Such a thing had never been heard of by him or his fathers, or any of the neighboring chiefs, or, in fact, anybody in Central Africa. But his little world was but a segment of a vaster circle.

So David Hume's experience and the experience of the world as he had traced it and observed it was by no means conclusive as to the complete facts even of nature itself. There was a larger circle that he had not compassed, and within that circle the facts of miracles are as real as the facts of the ordinary operations of nature on the lower plane. In fact, some day we will probably find that even miracles are but the operation of the higher laws on a divine plan which we have not understood, that it is the letting down for a moment of the forces of that spiritual realm which some day will be our natural sphere.

But the facts themselves when demonstrated by satisfactory evidences are conclusive seals and attestations of the truth of the testimony which appeals to God through these credentials. Christ distinctly appealed to the works that He did as the evidences of His divine character and the truth of His teachings, and we cannot imagine God, if He be a holy God, answering this appeal and bearing witness to His testimony if it were not true.

The maker and custodian of the great clock in Strasburg Cathedral had a grave misunderstanding with the authorities of the cathedral. Finding them unwilling to yield he quietly touched a spring in the tower and the clock stopped moving. The people wondered, questioned, complained and protested. The authorities employed mechanics and experts and skilled artisans in vain. Nobody could understand the works or make the clock go until at last they were obliged to appeal to the maker and yield to his terms. Then he quietly touched the spring again and the whole mechanism began to move. Because he was the maker he could arrest it and he could restore its operations.

And so there is but one Hand that can suspend the mighty wheels of nature's complicated mechanism, and there is but one Hand that can restore the power when interrupted. And when we see that Hand put forth to close the heavens at the word of Elijah, and then to open the brazen skies and send forth the copious showers at the same prophetic word, we know that He is bearing witness to the word of His servant. When we see the waves stilled, the sick healed, the dead raised, the very Son of God Himself come forth from the sealed tomb, with the distinct affirmation that these are the very credentials claimed by the witnesses who have given to us this Word, what but obstinate and inveterate blindness can doubt that this is indeed the authorized message of heaven, the Word of the living God?

2. Prophecy

The shrewdness of the human intellect may succeed in guessing with some degree of probability about the future. But there is an infinite distance between the boldest and wisest guesses of heathen oracles or human sages and the clear, decided predictions of the Holy Scriptures.

The criteria of prophecy are exceedingly simple and obvious:

First, the event predicted must be at a sufficient distance in the future.

Second, the predictions must be explicit and marked by points of identification about which there can be no mistake, such as locality, circumstances, names and so forth.

Third, there must be no apparent cause or train of circumstances that might bring about the event in question which could be known to the author of the prediction.

Fourth, the fulfillment must be open, public and sufficiently witnessed to render all deception impossible.

These are but a few of the tests of prophecy which distinguish them from the guesses of human wisdom, and in these respects the Scriptural prophecies shine in the meridian sunlight of truth.

Let us look for a moment at three classes of prophecies. First, there are the prophecies concerning the nations and political systems of the world. Centuries before the time of their fulfillment a number of prophetic witnesses, including such men as Isaiah, Jeremiah and Daniel, foretold the actual order of the world's great empires, the rise and fall of Babylon, Medo-Persia, Greece, Rome, and the political and ecclesiastical systems that were to come out of Rome. A perfect panorama of the political future of the world was laid out, and all the centuries since have been literally fulfilling it. Now, how could any human guess have ever foreshadowed these stupendous results? The events were too far in the distance to render them probable, and the fulfillment has been open in the face of the universe.

The same conclusion would be reached if we had time to take up in detail special prophecies concerning the fall of Nineveh, the capture of Babylon, the career of Cyrus, the history of nations like Edom, Egypt and Tyre, in the light of which we see a divine presence and exact fulfillment.

The second class of prophecies is concerning the Jews. As long ago as the time of Moses and down through the whole Old Testament, there is a clear line of prophecy pointing out the great facts of their national history, their supremacy among the nations, their fall under the power of the Gentile conquerors, their captivity on account of their sins, their rejection of the Messiah, their dispersion among all nations, their preservation distinct from all other peoples, their restoration ultimately to their own land.

How manifestly all this meets the test already given. There was nothing likely to lead up to that. The fulfillment has been open as the day, and so marked has been their providential history that when the great statesman was asked by one of the sovereigns of Europe what argument he could give for the truth of Christianity his simple answer was, "The Jews, your majesty, the Jews."

The third great class of prophecies are those respecting the Lord Jesus Christ. How explicitly, how exactly the ancient prophecies point out all the circumstances attending His first and second advent, His name, His birth of a virgin mother, the very place of His birth—Bethlehem, His rejection by His countrymen, His life of humility and suffering, His betrayal for 30 pieces of silver, His crucifixion and all the attending circumstances of His death, His resurrection, His coming again. So complete was the chain of Messianic prophecy that the evangelist stops to note at every stage of the last sad drama of His agony how each incident that happened was "that the scripture . . . be fulfilled" (John 19:24, 28, 36). So perfect is the picture that we could construct a biography of Christ from the Old Testament prophecies alone. Who can answer this mighty weight of prophetic testimony? Who can challenge this divine vindication of God's supernatural Book? Who can hesitate to say with holy veneration and humble faith, "Your word, O LORD, is eternal; it stands firm in the heavens" (Psalm 119:89).

3. The Life and Character of the Lord Jesus Christ

The story of Jesus is the mightiest proof of the truth of the Gospels. Such a story is absolutely without any explanation unless it is literally true.

Such a character is to us a miracle, and for any human mind to conceive it, invent it, to unfold it in these records would be a literary achievement so stupendous that the author would deserve to be immortalized as himself divine.

Who conceived this marvelous ideal? Whose brain originated this stupendous Book, if it was but a book? As Rousseau has well said, the creation of such a fiction would have been a greater miracle than to believe the fact itself to be true.

Dr. Fisher has forcibly said that this character is original. The world had nothing like it before. It is a blending of all the elements at once of gentleness and strength, of intellectual force and moral perfection, of self-surrender and yet sublime dignity and self-respect. There is no weakness about it, and yet there is no hardness, no selfishness, no pride, no despotic ambition to aggrandize Himself at the expense of others, like all the heroes of human history. It is evidently a sinless and spotless and perfect character. There is not a single failure anywhere. The ideal is sustained throughout consistently with itself, and even in the very tragedy of His death there is a moral sublimity and a triumph of character greater even than earthly success.

Then it is to be noticed that this character is not a study of literary skill, wrought up with any preconceived plan to create an ideal, but it is developed incidentally out of a thousand common occurrences in actual life, unfolding day by day and evidently as unforeseen by the writers as by us. It all grows up naturally out of facts as they develop and it bears upon its very surface the impression of simplicity, genuineness and absolute reality. No man can candidly read these Gospel narratives and not feel that he is standing in the presence of a life that is supernatural and divine, and the book that records it must be the Word of God.

Even the great Napoleon remarked, "I think I understand somewhat of human nature, and I tell you all these were men, and I am a man, but not one is like Him. Jesus Christ was more than a man. Alexander, Caesar, Charlemagne and myself founded great empires, but upon what did the creation of our genius depend but on force? Jesus alone founded His empire upon love, and to this day millions would die for Him. The gospel is no mere book, but a living creature, with a power which conquers all that possess it. Here lies the Book of books upon this table."

4. The Influence of This Book

It has revolutionized human society. It has civilized the nations that have accepted it. It is the secret of the greatness and power of the Protestant nations. It goes into the heathen populations, and lo, a cannibal of the South Sea islands is transformed into a gentle Christian, a warring Indian anarchist becomes a peaceful disciple of Christ, a selfish Asian merchant develops into a heroic martyr, and a downtrodden African villager rises to the noblest type of manhood. The polygamist gives up his wives, the sorcerer gives up his superstitions, thousands of men and women become outcasts from their homes and often martyrs for their faith, and the whole phase of human society is stamped with the uplifting impress and the heavenly influence of the Book of God.

Skepticism is well enough to laugh and talk about, but, as Voltaire once said when his infidel friends were discussing their theories at his dining table, "Hush gentlemen, till the servants are gone. If they believed as we do none of our lives would be safe."

5. Experiential Evidence

The experience of the child of God, and the internal evidence which it brings to every heart that receives it on its own terms with obedience and trust is the final evidence of the supernatural nature of this Book. Like the Jewish tabernacle which was very coarse and common looking on the outside, but whose beauties could only be seen from within, this blessed Book must be loved to be understood and appreciated. It speaks to the spirit of the child of God with an assurance that awakens the spontaneous sensibilities of his renewed being, and answers like the people of Samaria, "We have heard for ourselves, and we know that this man really is the Savior of the world" (John 4:42).

If you want to know that this Book is true, meet it on its own terms. Take it to your heart, read it with simplicity and candor, test it by obedience, and you will find it is all it claims to be.

In a city where I once was a pastor there was a brilliant lawyer who, with his young wife, attended my ministry. She was a devoted Christian. He was a notorious skeptic, and was recognized as the leading free thinker of the community. I knew it was vain to argue with him, but many hearts were praying for him. At last this lovely girl died. A few days after her death he sent for me to his office, and in a very frank way immediately began to tell me that he had just become a Christian. I was quite surprised, and asked him how it happened.

"Well," he said, "I have read everything on the subject for years, and I never could reach a conclusion. As I read one side of the argument I was partly convinced, but when I read the other the balance turned, and I never seemed quite able to decide between the two. The brain was not strong enough to balance these weights, and so I have been all my life in a state of honest indecision. But while my wife lived with me I saw in her something which I did not possess, and something that I knew to be real; and when she died I saw that it was worth all that I possessed and in the agony of my bereavement I suddenly found myself one day praying to her God. Instantly my reason came to me and protested, and I said to myself, why are you praying to somebody you don't believe in; but before I could stop it the prayer had got into heaven and God had answered it, and something came to my heart that I had never felt before. It was the touch of the supernatural Presence, and it was so exquisite and comforting that I just kept on praying; God kept on answering until this very moment. Although I cannot explain it, I cannot justify it by my reason, yet I know that it is true. I know that it is God and I am a Christian, not through my head, but through my heart."

That is the secret of faith. That is the supreme test. Dare to test it.

> Oh, make but trial of His word,
>   Experience will decide
> How happy they and only they
>   Who in His truth confide.

When you cannot understand the Bible through your brain, take it in your soul, press it to your heart, bring to it your sorrow, your sin, your need; and you will know it is true because it has searched you, it has converted you, and it has satisfied you.

A blind girl lay dying and her paralyzed fingers had ceased to be able to read by touch the raised letters of her precious Bible. With a sad cry she dropped it, and she said, "My precious Bible, I cannot feel any more the touch of your precious promises." Then in an impulse of passionate love she pressed it to her lips to say goodbye, when suddenly she gave a great cry of joy, and she said, "I can read it still; I can feel it with my lips." She pressed it again and again, page after page, to her sensitive lips as she drank in its consolations, and went to sleep with her head pillowed upon its heavenly promises.

Beloved, when all other senses fail, you can read and understand the Bible with your love. It is not a Book for intellectual discussions or brilliant exhibitions of our exegetical acuteness. It is a Book to love! It is a Book to translate into living copies and holy example.

"Each of us is either a Bible or a libel." Let us reverence it. Let us believe it. Let us love it. Let us live it. Let us give it to a perishing world.

> Eternal are Thy mercies, Lord;
> Eternal truth attends Thy Word;
> Thy praise shall sound from shore to shore.
> Till suns shall rise and set no more.

CHAPTER 3

The Supernatural Life

*I no longer live, but Christ lives in me.
(Galatians 2:20)*

The best edition of the Holy Scriptures is a holy life. God wants to translate His supernatural Book into the living experience of all His children.

When someone said to Sir Walter Scott that he was going to write a book, he answered, "Be a book."

When the enemies of the apostles saw the man who had been healed standing in their midst they could say nothing against it. A living, consistent Bible Christian is an unanswerable witness for God and evidence for Christianity in every age. Christ Himself was the greatest miracle of the Gospels and so every Christian should be greater than all his works.

The radical distinction between Christianity and all other religions is in the characters that it produces. "By their fruit you will recognize them" (Matthew 7:16) is Christ's own test. Judged by this test, Christianity is unanswerable. The Christian character is not the product of moral culture. The holiest men are the readiest to acknowledge that in them dwells no good thing, and that every virtue and grace is due alone to the power of the divine Presence as it dwells within them and strengthens them against their temptations and weaknesses.

The Fact of Justification

The first supernatural fact in the Christian life is a divine righteousness or what is termed in the language of theology, justification. The Apostle Paul uses a very fine phrase in unfolding this fundamental principle of the gospel by which man becomes right with God. He calls it the righteousness of God. It is not merely the mercy of God overlooking our fall but it is the righteousness of God settling our account and putting us right with Him. God wants us to stand approved in His presence—not by our own works, but by the imputed righteousness of the Lord Jesus Christ. God meets us at the very threshold when we come guilty, condemned, unworthy and excluded from His favor and His presence. He clothes us in the very merits of His own Son, enabling us thus to look in the face of the very throne and even of the victims and witnesses of our crimes and know that we are without blame, justified and counted righteous in His sight and standing in the same attitude as if we had never sinned. This is the free gift of God—holy, supernatural and divine. We are clothed in God's own righteousness and while we have nothing of our own to boast, yet we can look up in the blessed light of the throne and say,

> Jesus, Thy blood and righteousness
>   My beauty are, my glorious dress.
> Sinless with these garments on
>   I'll face the splendors of Thy throne.

The Fact of Regeneration

The second supernatural fact of a Christian life is regeneration. This is quite different from justification. The latter makes our relations right with God. The former makes our nature right. It is the divine impartation to the human being of a new life communicated directly from God—pure and holy as His own very being. This is not moral elevation, self-improvement, doing or being better, but a miracle of grace, a new creation, a wonder so stupendous that Nicodemus, a Jewish professor of ethics and religion, could not comprehend it but looked with wonder in the face of Christ and asked how these things could be.

There is nothing parallel to it in nature. Perhaps the nearest analogy to it is the little ichneumon that deposits its tiny eggs through the coarse skin of the caterpillar in its body and leaves them there to hatch in the warm temperature of its victim until they germinate and, feeding upon the flesh of the caterpillar, grow to maturity and then burst the shell and spring into life.

But the ichneumon is a natural progenitor of this germ of life. In regeneration there is no human power that can propagate this life. No man can give it to his brother. No parent can communicate it to his child. "Children born not of natural descent, nor of human decision or a husband's will, but born of God" (John 1:13). The feeblest saint is a new order of being, in the eyes of the angels as marvelous as when Adam stepped out upon the theater of Eden, "while the morning stars sang together and all the angels shouted for joy" (Job 38:7).

The Fact of Sonship

The next supernatural fact in the Christian life is sonship. We enter at once into the heavenly family. This, too, is a surpassing wonder and quite contrary to the precedents of the divine government. Angels were very high in the scale of being, but they dared not enter the family of God; yet sinful man stepped across the threshold of the palace and the prodigal came home to his Father's bosom and claimed a place no archangel can ever know. "How great is the love the Father has lavished on us, that we should be called children of God!" (1 John 3:1) was the cry of John, the man who stood nearest to the very center of the throne.

We are the sons of God by virtue of our being

born of God. We are not only "called" but we "are" the sons of God. Not only are we sons by a decree of adoption but every intuition of the new heart leaps to meet the Father and knows its own delightful place of filial recognition, for we have "received the Spirit of sonship. And by him we cry, '*Abba*, Father' " (Romans 8:15).

We have a still higher claim to sonship by virtue of our union with Christ, the only begotten Son of God. Wedded to Him, we come into His peculiar sonship. And so we are called the firstborn ones, the very name that He holds. As a bride inherits her husband's home and is accepted as a child, so we go in with Him to the innermost chambers of the palace of the King while we hear Him say, "My Father and your Father, . . . my God and your God" (John 20:17).

The Fact of Christ's Indwelling

The indwelling of Christ is the next supernatural fact into which we are brought. This is a transition as stupendous as regeneration itself. "If anyone loves me," Christ says, "he will obey my teaching. My Father will love him, and we will come to him and make our home with him" (14:23). This is not a figure but a fact so glorious and real that the Apostle Paul declared it to be the very secret which had been hid from ages and from generations but which at last had been made known to the saints and which was committed to him to give as a talisman of the victory and the secret of heaven's own life to the children of God.

The Fact of the Baptism of the Holy Spirit

The baptism of the Holy Spirit is the fifth supernatural fact of our life. While the same in its effects substantially as the indwelling of Christ and while it is through the Holy Spirit that we come into union with Him, yet it is a distinct privilege and experience of the Christian life. The prophet Ezekiel, in describing the experience of a converted soul, after telling of the new heart and the new spirit that He would put within them adds this higher promise, "And I will put my Spirit in you and move you to follow my decrees and be careful to keep my laws" (Ezekiel 36:27). God's own Spirit comes into the new spirit. It is not only that we have a new heart but we have the Almighty God residing in that new heart. So stupendous was the change which this brought to the apostles after the day of Pentecost that all men took knowledge of them that they had been with Jesus. They were clothed with a new power. They were invested with a divine authority and efficiency by which their words brought conviction to the consciences of men, and the works of the risen Christ were wrought through their hands, and all men felt a supernatural presence and power around them and upon them.

A supernatural holiness becomes a fact of our lives, for sanctification is not our personal virtues, graces or attainments, but it is the life of Christ manifested in us. The finest definition of it is given by Paul in First Corinthians 1:30-31: "It is because of him that you are in Christ Jesus, who has become for us wisdom from God—that is, our righteousness, holiness and redemption. Therefore, as it is written: 'Let him who boasts boast in the Lord.' "

Sanctification is here distinctly recognized not as our character but as the inworking and the outworking of Christ's own life in us. He is made unto us of God our righteousness, our sanctification just in order that we may not glory in our own goodness but may recognize everything we are and do as the grace of Christ.

This is the same thought expressed by John in his Gospel where he says, "From the fullness of his grace we have all received one blessing after another [grace for grace, KJV]" (John 1:16). That is, His grace gives to us the supply which constitutes the different graces in us. Do we want humility? We take Christ's Spirit within us to be the spirit of humility. Do we want patience and love? We put on Christ as our patience and love and He works out in us and relives through us His own longsuffering, unselfish life. Out of His fullness we thus receive even "grace for grace" and when the work is accomplished we do not stand before our fellow men as paragons and patterns of superiority, but examples of the free and sovereign grace which they may have as well as we.

Not only does Christ give us a supernatural supply but a supernatural standard of holiness. In this respect Christianity differs from all human ethics. Chinese morality had crystallized itself in a proverb not unlike our golden rule though not nearly so clear and strong. But even the golden rule does not express the highest standard of New Testament holiness. "Love your neighbor as yourself" (Leviticus 19:18) is the Old Testament morality; "A new command I give you: Love one another. As I have loved you, so you must love one another" (John 13:34). This is the supernatural standard of Christianity. "Be perfect, therefore, as your heavenly Father is perfect" (Matthew 5:48). This is an aim transcending the highest dream of the world's teachers. "Love your enemies, do good to those who hate you, bless those who curse you, pray for those who mistreat you" (Luke 6:27-28).

This, when exemplified in living obedience, awes the human heart and convicts it of a power superhuman and divine.

Divine guidance is one of the supernatural privileges of the Christian life. For every consecrated soul God has a distinct plan and a divine program lifting it above all common lives and making it marked and sublime. It may be a very simple life and exercised in a very humble sphere but the fact that God is shaping, molding and using it gives to it a dignity unspeakably high. The life of a Joseph, the life of an Esther, the life of a Paul is a romance of providence, and every one of us may possess such a charmed life and know that God has made of us a pattern of our earthly temple and is building better than we know.

When the great Hildebrand was dying, he told

some of his friends that the secret of his life was that he had taken St. Peter as the patron saint of his whole career and that all along the way he felt that the influence of this mighty spirit was directing all his ways. How much better for us to take Peter's Master as the pattern of our life and let Him so possess it that He will have a loving pride in making out of us the very best possible for a trusting soul and a human career.

Along with this it may be added that divine providence enters directly into the life of the child of God. Especially is this true when our whole life is dedicated to God and conformed to His high calling. Then for us the promise becomes true, "in all things God works for the good of those who love him, who have been called according to his purpose" (Romans 8:28). This is not true in the same sense of every Christian but only of those who are living according to His purpose, as stated in the context, "to be conformed to the likeness of his Son" (8:29).

If that is the character of our life and if we thus truly love and live for God with the singleness and strength of an undivided heart, we will find that all the wheels of providence move at the touch of the Hand that is leading us.

How wonderful is the story of providence in God's Word and especially in the lives of those who truly belonged to God. He ruled and overruled in the stories of Joseph, Moses, Nehemiah, Daniel, Philip in his meeting with the eunuch in the desert and Peter in his marvelous deliverance from prison while his pursuer was stricken in the same hour by the hand of God. How inadequately we realize and claim that overshadowing promise that covers all our way, "All authority in heaven and on earth has been given to me. . . . And surely I am with you always, to the very end of the age" (Matthew 28:18, 20). How often we forget that the affairs of nations and even the business of the world moves simply for the sake of Christ and His people. He is Head over all things for His body, the Church. Our vast political systems and commercial activities are but the agencies through which He is preparing the way for the witnessing of the gospel and the evangelization of the world. Oh, to ride forth with Him in His chariot and see Him triumph over all our enemies and His! This is the supernatural privilege of the sons of God and the service of Christ.

There is no wonder more supernatural and divine in the life of the believer than the mystery and the ministry of prayer. The mighty statesman Daniel turned away from his official task and the courtly visitors that awaited him, and for three whole weeks was prostrate on his face in prayer before the throne of a greater king than Cyrus. As he prayed, the earth's mightiest conqueror was unable to sleep. He called for the archives of his kingdom and the records respecting the Jews, and when the morning dawned, sent for his scribe and dictated this decree: "The LORD, the God of heaven, has given me all the kingdoms of the earth and he has appointed me to build a temple for him at Jerusalem in Judah. Anyone of his people among you—may the LORD his God be with him, and let him go up" (2 Chronicles 36:23).

How did this heathen conqueror know about the Lord Jehovah? What did he care for Israel's God? What cared he for fear or favor respecting the little captive bands of Israel in his land? What but a touch from the throne could put such a thought in his heart or such language on his lips? Ah, it was the answer to Daniel's prayer. It was the moving of a scepter which is touched in the silent closet. Those captive bands arose and started forth on their homeward way with Zerubbabel, Ezra and Nehemiah; the temple was raised from its ruins; the city walls were restored; the ages rolled on until the Son of God Himself preached the gospel of the kingdom. The vision given Daniel in answer to his prayer does not close until the latest ages have all rolled by and the course of empires is finished and the vision of prophecy fulfilled and the times of the Gentiles ended and the Lord Himself has come.

Wonder of wonders! Mystery of mysteries! Miracle of miracles! The hand of the child touching the arm of the Father moves the wheels of the universe. Beloved, this is your supernatural place and mine, and over its gates we read this inspiring invitation, "Call to me and I will answer you and tell you great and unsearchable things you do not know" (Jeremiah 33:3).

CHAPTER 4

The Supernatural Church

Christ loved the church and gave himself up for her to make her holy, cleansing her by the washing with water through the word, and to present her to himself as a radiant church, without stain or wrinkle or any other blemish, but holy and blameless. (Ephesians 5:25-27)

There is a social and collective element in our human life, and therefore, Christianity involves not only a supernatural man but a divine society. Adam represented the race as a whole and Christ also has a people who are bound together by certain ties of life and fellowship and united under certain common characteristics as an organic whole.

Early in the story of the human race we find humanity divided into two great societies. One is called the sons and daughters of men, developing in the family of Cain, the other the sons of God, connected with the family of Seth.

Immediately after these two lines separate we

find this remarkable statement in Genesis 4:26: "At that time men began to call on the name of the LORD." More correctly this passage may be translated, "At that time men began to call themselves by the name of the LORD." This was the organization of a divine society and it was organized with a divine name. They called themselves by the very name of the Lord as God's own special people.

In beautiful harmony with this we find in the early chapters of the New Testament that the society of believers also took a special name. This was the name of Christ. "The disciples were called Christians first at Antioch" (Acts 11:26) and it has been happily suggested by one that this name was probably given not merely by the world around them but assumed by themselves as linking them more closely and directly with Christ. They were a divine society—Christ ones, literally.

Now, the Church of Jesus Christ is a divine society and there is no truth that has more need of emphasis in these days of compromise than the supernatural character and destiny of the Church of the Lord Jesus. Christ Himself announced its heavenly character before He left the world, as, referring to His own divinity, He declared, "On this rock I will build my church, and the gates of Hades will not overcome it" (Matthew 16:18).

In the later teachings of the Holy Spirit through the inspired apostles the doctrine of the Church is unfolded with great fullness and the fundamental principles of this divine society are brought out with great clearness under the three striking figures of the building, the body and the bride.

Called by His Name

The Church has a divine Head. "For no one can lay any foundation other than the one already laid, which is Jesus Christ" (1 Corinthians 3:11). So intimately is He connected with it that in the 12th chapter of First Corinthians, the great chapter of the Church, it is even called by His very name, not the Church of Christ, but Christ: "The body is a unit, though it is made up of many parts; and though all its parts are many, they form one body. So it is with Christ" (12:12). He identifies Himself here with the Church just as a man is identified with his own body.

No human name is big enough to dominate the Church. No single doctrine is important enough to give name and character to the Church of Christ. Methods have their place, but that place is not important enough to constitute a Methodist church. Baptism is very dear to every believer in the Bible, but baptism is not near enough the center to justify the establishment of the Baptist church. Presbyterianism recognizes the equality of the ministry but even this is not of sufficient consequence to substitute for the name of Jesus the name of Presbyterian. Episcopacy recognizes the dignity of the bishop and the sacredness of the government of the Church but an Episcopal church is a lower name than the dignity of

Christ's Church demands.

It is well for us to recognize in the life and fellowship of Christ all these sections of the circle, but it would be much more to the honor of Christ if all were lost in His all-glorious name. He is the Head of the Church. He alone should govern and control it. He alone should be its end and aim, its all in all.

The Church has a divine constitution. "See to it that you make everything according to the pattern shown you on the mountain" (Hebrews 8:5) was the law of the ancient tabernacle and it applies to the Church of which that tabernacle was the type.

Man cannot construct a church according to his theories and preferences. God has settled the question of its worship, ordinances and membership, and any society which claims to be a church and is not founded upon a regenerated membership, the inspiration of the Word and that supernatural presence, power and authority of the Lord Jesus Christ, may be a Sunday club or a literary Lyceum—but it is not the Church of the Lord Jesus Christ.

The Church has a supernatural life. We must be born into the Church. We cannot be added to it. We are added to Him, as the passage in Acts (2:41) literally should be translated, and that adds us to the Church.

"For we were all baptized by one Spirit"—or rather, *in* one Spirit—"into one body—whether Jews or Greeks, slave or free—and we were all given the one Spirit to drink" (1 Corinthians 12:13). It is not only *by* the Holy Spirit, but *in* the Holy Spirit that we are united to the Church. A simple figure will illustrate the difference between the two prepositions.

That ship in the sea is connected with the sea, but not part of it. They are distinct substances. But it is very different with the mighty river, the Hudson, which this moment is flowing into the sea and is now merged in the sea. The Hudson is part of the sea. It is blended with it; they are one.

That is the way we become members of the Church. We partake of the common life of the body through the Holy Spirit.

This was brought out in the typical story of Eve's birth and marriage. She was made out of Adam with a common life, and then she was given back to Adam to be his bride.

So the Church is born out of Christ's life, and then put back into Christ's arms as His beloved.

Nothing less than this supernatural life can ever constitute true membership in Christ's Church. Sacraments will not do it. Subscriptions to the Church funds will not do it. Official position will not do it. The laying on of hands and rites of ordination or confirmation will not do it. It is a heaven-born oneness—a unity of life.

In the Church of Ephesus there was a fine organization; there was a great deal of work. There was a great zeal for orthodoxy and a deliberate hunting down of heretics; but, notwithstanding all this, Christ was so grieved and even disgusted that He was about to remove the candlestick of Ephesus out of its place simply because they had left their first love and their life, as He literally expressed it respecting another of these churches, was "about to die" (Revelation 3:2).

Not of This World

The Church has a supernatural object. She is not an earthly kingdom, but a heavenly people. As truly as her Master can she say, "My kingdom is not of this world" (John 18:36). What has she to do with vast endowments, social preeminence, parliaments of religion, mayoralty contests, political campaigns and royal patronage? It is hers to go "up from the desert, leaning on her lover" (Song of Songs 8:5). It is the mark of the false, earthly, apostate church that she is seen sitting on the beast of earthly power, allied to the arm of flesh, and bearing as her seal the boastful legend, "She sits supreme over all the world" (see Revelation 17).

The beginning of the great apostasy was the ambition of the first prelates and bishops of the early Church to have the foremost place in the banquets of the Emperor. And that little strife about who should go in first to dinner or stand in the Church was the beginning of the very papacy itself.

Alas, even in our democratic age the bribe of the world's favor and the popular applause of the multitude has proved as fatal to the Church's purity and left her with Laodicea, which means to "please the people," basking in the smiles of the world, but standing on the very verge of the awful and impending judgment of her indignant and insulted Lord.

What are the great objects of the Church of Christ? First, she must worship God and glorify her Father in heaven. Second, she must bear witness to the truth. She is called the pillar and crown of truth—that is, as the pillar supports the archway with its inscription, so the Church is called to uphold the great archway of revelation and hold before the world the testimony of God. And therefore her heavenly object is propagation, evangelization, to gather to her bosom the sinful world, to instruct and build them up in the life of Jesus, to be the training school for heaven and to give the gospel to all mankind. This is her heavenly calling. She is the only divine society on earth, the only institution that is essential and eternal, the only one that will survive the wreck of time and the dissolution of the present age. Let us understand her high calling and oh, let her be true to it!

The Church's Source of Power

The Church is endowed with supernatural powers. To her is given the baptism of the Holy Spirit. In her abides the living heart of Christ while the Head sits upon the mediatorial throne controlling all things for her good.

Christianity differs in this from all other systems. Each of them had a head, but the heart is cold to death. The heart of Christianity is the

Holy Spirit living still in all the omnipotence of God in the bosom of the Church and quickening her with her Master's risen life. It is He that uses her testimony to "convict the world of . . . sin and righteousness and judgment" (John 16:8). It is He who clothes her messages with "the power of God for the salvation of everyone who believes" (Romans 1:16). It is He who gives wisdom to her leaders and efficiency to her plans. It is His presence that separates her from all other societies, and makes this her distinguishing glory, as Moses said of Israel of old. Her object is not to lean on mighty intellects or large wealthy, powerful organizations, but upon the living God.

And He has clothed her with supernatural powers in the physical realm. When John sent to Jesus for the credentials of His ministry the answer given was, "Go back and report to John what you hear and see: The blind receive sight, the lame walk, those who have leprosy are cured, the deaf hear, the dead are raised, and the good news is preached to the poor" (Matthew 11:4-5). These are still Christ's confirmatory signs for His true Church. God forgive her for having so long surrendered them! God help her to reclaim them in these last days, to keep them in their true place and yet never to ignore them. They are like the jewels on Rebekah's robes, the earthly insignia of Isaac's love. Her robe is holiness; her jewels are the gifts of power.

Christ intended that His Church should embrace all forms of ministry for all classes of need—the sick, the orphan, the stranger, the poor, the ignorant, the lost. Oh, for the revival of apostolic and primitive Church life! Oh, for the vision of the woman clothed with the sun, crowned with stars and the moon, the lower light of earth's midnight, under her feet (Revelation 12:1)!

The Church has a supernatural support. The ascended Christ with all the resources of His providential government is her Head and Light. As He sends her forth her all-sufficient guarantee is this: "All authority in heaven and on earth has been given to me.... And surely I am with you always" (Matthew 28:18, 20).

As the bride of the Lamb and the co-heir of all His boundless wealth, what business has she to go about with her hat in her hand begging the petty pittance of their gifts from the brewers, distillers, gamblers and speculators of the earth, selling tickets for strawberry festivals, broom drills and indescribable follies of every kind and vainly competing with the literary lecture bureau or with the cheap theater for platform entertainments to draw the masses, and sometimes stoop even to the promiscuous dance to attract visitors to her Sunday school picnic or help out the deficiency in the preacher's salary? God convict her and God deliver her!

A Calling from God

The Church has a supernatural destiny. Her calling is to be the glorious Church, and some day when He presents her to Himself "without stain or wrinkle or any other blemish" (Ephesians 5:27), bright with all the glory of the apocalyptic vision of the New Jerusalem, brightest of all with the reflected light and beauty of her Bridegroom and her Head, she will be the wonder of the universe; and they will come from every star to gaze upon her while the attendant angels will say, "Come, I will show you the bride, the wife of the Lamb" (Revelation 21:9).

A beautiful old legend intimates that in the very center of man's first paradise was a temple of gems, where Adam worshiped God in the days of his unfallen innocence. Its floor was of shining gold and its walls were of carbuncles, jaspers, rubies, emeralds and amethysts; its dome was a blazing diamond. But in the ruin of the fall that temple was torn to fragments and all the pieces scattered over the earth, and today we find them in little broken gems in the hearts of the mountains and in the depths of oceans. By and by, the legend tells us, in the age to come they are to be crystallized again into a yet more glorious temple, the vision of John, the New Jerusalem.

Well, whatever the legend amounts to, at least, we know that the children of God today are scattered, like jeweled fragments, in every race and clime, but they are gems of unparalleled preciousness and value. Next to Christ, the most precious thing on earth is Christ's people.

All our work here is but imperfect. Builders are like Solomon's workmen in the mountains, sending off one by one the stones and timbers but not seeing the building yet. The Church will rise in silent majesty as Solomon's temple rose, and as we look upon its stately splendor, its external foundations, its celestial towers, its glorious brightness, its supernal light, we will not be sorry for the toils and tears we gladly gave and the song we often sang:

> I love Thy kingdom, Lord,
>   The house of Thine abode,
> The Church our blessed Redeemer bought
>   With His own precious blood.

In conclusion, let us never dwarf the glorious conception of the Church of Jesus by identifying it only with our little sectarian conceptions. Let us love and cherish every branch of the true Church of God, but let us rise above them all to the divine conception, and in all our fellowships, associations and alliances let us steadily hold that great communion of saints which is part of the Apostle's Creed and the eternal hope. It has been said: "We are not come-outers. We are come-uppers and go-outers." Stripped of its colloquialism it just means, lift the Church higher and carry the gospel further to a dying world, and so hasten the day when He will come to the general assembly and Church of the firstborn ones who are written in heaven, to the New Jerusalem and innumerable company of angels, to God, the Judge of all, and "the spirits of righteous men made perfect" (Hebrews 12:23).

CHAPTER 5

The Supernatural Body

And if the Spirit of him who raised Jesus from the dead is living in you, he who raised Christ from the dead will also give life to your mortal bodies through his Spirit, who lives in you. (Romans 8:11)

The redemption of the body is an accepted truth of Christianity. The chief difference among Christians is with respect to the extent of its application. Many believe that this part of our redemption is only to be realized at the close of the present age in the translation and resurrection at the coming of our Lord. Others of us have been led to believe that we anticipate in the present life to a certain extent the power of our future resurrection, and that we have a foretaste of heaven.

This, we believe, is what is meant by the use of the word "earnest" (2 Corinthians 1:22, 5:5, Ephesians 1:14, KJV) or "firstfruits" (Romans 8:23) applied in several instances in relation to the work of the Holy Spirit in our bodies. An earnest is a first installment, a pledge in kind of the thing which is afterward to be given in full. As the earnest of our spiritual future, He gives us in our spirit the foretaste of the heavenly glory; as the earnest of the resurrection of the body, He gives us the physical life of Christ in our mortal body. He anticipates in our material form now, as far as we are able to receive it, that which we will enjoy in boundless fullness in the body of glory in the ages to come.

An earnest is the very same in kind but less in degree than that of which it is the pledge. Therefore, if the Holy Spirit is to be the earnest of our physical resurrection, it must be through some physical operation in our being now.

We believe that we will have a supernatural body in the heavenly world, but we also believe that we begin to receive the elements of that body now, if not its form at least its vital element and the hidden power which is to animate it then.

The Blessing Is for Today

We are always putting forward God's blessings to some future time instead of accepting them now, if not its form at least its vital element and the hidden power which is to animate it then. We are like poor Martha who, when our Lord had said to her, "Your brother will rise again," timidly pushed it forward to the distant future and answered, "I know he will rise again . . . at the last day." Jesus gently reproved her error and answered quickly, "I am the resurrection and the life" (John 11:23-25). It was as if He had said, "Martha, do not postpone the blessing your faith would claim but take Me for it now. The resurrection when it comes will come through Me and where I am there is the power of the resurrection. I am speaking to you in the present tense; I have for you a present blessing." Then He proceeded to expand the thought in every direction that we have been explaining. "He who believes in me will live, even though he dies; and whoever lives and believes in me will never die" (11:25-26).

He seems clearly to teach us that believing in Him we receive the life which passes through death to us, or rather rises above it and lives on forever, tunneling through the dark of the tomb and passing on in unbroken, uninterrupted being into the larger life beyond.

This then is the truth which we desire to unfold from the Holy Scriptures, that we may possess even now, through the Lord Jesus Christ, a measure of supernatural life and strength in our mortal frame sufficient to enable us for all the pressures and duties of this life and sustain us until our life's work is done.

We see some foreshadowings of this great truth in the story of the fall. In consequence of sin man was instantly debarred from the tree of life, which was the symbol and source of his physical immortality. But while this supply of perpetual physical life was withdrawn it was not forever precluded, for God erected at the gate of Eden a glorious medium of approach to His presence described as the cherubim and the flaming sword "which turned every way, to keep the way of the tree of life" (Genesis 3:24, KJV).

This symbolic figure of the cherubim and the sword we do not believe are emblems of divine judgment so much as of divine mercy. The Hebrew verb here is *Shekinah*; literally, He "shekinahed" the cherubim and flaming sword. We know that the Shekinah and the cherubim as they reappear in the later symbols of the tabernacle were tokens of the divine mercy and Jehovah's covenant with Israel, and we cannot but think that the fiery sword was some supernatural light, perhaps the Shekinah itself, which indicated the presence of God and the blessing on the worship.

That which we have associated with terror and repulsion was the first gate of mercy open for fallen man and the sense in which it was to "keep the way of the tree of life" might more properly be expressed by using the word "guard." It was to guard the way and to guide the way to the tree of life. From that tree sinful man was debarred on the natural plane, but he could now approach it on the higher plane of grace. His physical life was forfeited by his fall, but it could be won back again by the great redemption of which that cherubic sign was the glorious symbol.

We get back our lost strength now, not through nature but through the supernatural, not through the toil of Eden or the efforts of the flesh but through the Lord Jesus Christ, our redeeming Lord and our living Head.

Coming down the line of divine revelation we next meet with a distinct recognition of the supernatural life of God in our bodies in the story of Abraham, Sarah and Isaac. Here the strength of nature was allowed to fail before the seed of promise could be born. It was something like a foreshadowing of the birth of the Son of God which was not in a natural but in a supernatural way. Isaac, the seed of promise and the first type of the coming One, could not come into life until the natural life of his parents had withered and by a directly supernatural touch God had given new life even to their bodies.

Believing God for Your Body

This is what Paul meant in his description of Abraham's faith. We are told that he considered his body "as good as dead" (Romans 4:19) without being discouraged, for he was strong in faith, giving glory to God and looking directly to Him, by supernatural means, to make good that for which nature had no resources. Could there be a more signal and emphatic object lesson of the fact that God would lift the hearts of His people to a divine source even for the strength of our mortal frame? Could there be a more striking foreshadowing of the supernatural body which Christ has been preparing for the members of His mystical body?

The story of Israel was a significant illustration

of the supernatural physical life which God can give His children. All through the wilderness they were physically sustained by directly divine agencies. The very symbol of their life was a burning bush that burned and was not consumed (Exodus 3). This great sign which preceded Israel's call out of Egypt embodied in itself the idea of tremendous pressure overcome by infinite strength and divine protection. This was the story of the chosen people all the way through.

Indeed, Moses himself in reviewing it tells us that the very object of God in leading them as He did along the pilgrim way was to show them and teach them that "man does not live on bread alone but on every word that comes from the mouth of the LORD" (Deuteronomy 8:3). It was an illustration of a supernatural physical life while walking with God and drawing life directly from Him.

As this was true of the nation as a whole so it was also true of the most prominent individuals in the nation. Therefore we see that Moses' own life was distinctly supernatural. He began his great work at the age of 80 when most men would be writing their will and preparing for their funeral, and at the age of 120 we are told that his eye was not dimmed nor his natural force abated, but he calmly climbed a lofty mountain and in his full maturity stepped into the chariot of God and passed in victorious strength and voluntary surrender into the glory.

The life of Caleb was also supernatural. Surely

he had enough to break his heart and wear out his life in the strivings of a gainsaying people who kept him nearly half a century out of the promised land. But, when an old man of 85, we behold him standing before Joshua and asking as the choicest privilege of his life the opportunity of leading an assault upon the stronghold of the Canaanites, the old citadel of Hebron, and declaring, "I, however, followed the LORD my God wholeheartedly. . . . Now then, just as the LORD promised, he has kept me alive. . . . So here I am today, eight-five years old! I am still as strong today as the day Moses sent me out; I'm just as vigorous to go out to battle now as I was then" (Joshua 14:8, 10-11). He attributed his whole physical strength to the blessing of God and the blessed results of obedience and fidelity.

Physical Strength and Righteousness

But God has given us a still more distinct object lesson of this great principle of the supernatural body in the wonderful story of Samson. The one purpose of his life seems to have been to illustrate the connection between physical strength and rightness with God. When true to his Nazirite vow of separation and filled with the Spirit of God, he was a giant of unequaled muscular might. But when he broke his sacred vow of separation and lost the Holy Spirit he became as weak as unspun flax and sank helpless in the hands of his foes. Probably he did not lose an ounce of weight but he lost the secret of his strength, the life of the Holy Spirit. It is not the size of a wire that constitutes its strength. A little hair wire filled with an electric current is mightier than one of the cedars of Lebanon. It is the fluid that sweeps through it that makes it strong.

And so the supernatural life in which God is leading those who are willing to learn and to follow is not the result of physical culture but is the unfolding of the divine life and the anticipation of the unseen forces of the world to come.

The same great principle is illustrated in the story of David, who constantly recognized his military prowess, his courage and the strength of his victorious arm as due to the touch of God. He was clothed with a supernatural body and he could say of Jehovah, "He trains my hands for battle; my arms can bend a bow of bronze" (Psalm 18:34); "who . . . heals all your diseases, who redeems your life from the pit . . . who satisfies your desires with good things so that your youth is renewed like the eagle's" (Psalm 103:3-5).

But as we turn to the New Testament the very first view we obtain of the Lord Jesus Christ, our great Teacher and Example, is in this very connection. We see Him standing in the wilderness going through His first conflict with Satan and living out for us that great object lesson of our own life. The first of these temptations was a physical one, the temptation to secure His bodily strength from human sources. And how did He meet it? By the very passage we have already quoted from Deuteronomy, by the very lesson He had learned from the story of Israel in the wilderness. The devil was trying to persuade Him that He must get out of this strait by some means and that He must resort to earthly measures of relief. He replied by telling Satan, "Man does not live on bread alone, but on every word that comes from the mouth of God" (Matthew 4:4). He did not deny the place of the human and the earthly in supporting the life of man, but He did protest against being dependent upon the human and the earthly.

Bread has its true place but it is not "bread alone." There is something more for a man to say than "I must live." The true thing to say is, "I must meet God in my trial, I must learn my lesson, I must accomplish the purpose for which He has brought me here, and the purpose for which He has brought me here is to show that He is all-sufficient even for my body. I must stand there until this purpose is fulfilled. I must throw myself upon Him until He gives me relief and deliverance."

It is very significant that in this quotation Christ does not say the Son of Man but He says "man." It is very plain that He means the lesson for all His disciples. It is for us as well as Him.

Avoid the Extremes

It is true there is danger of extremes. All truth has its possibility of extravagance. There is a reckless disregard of the natural. God does not mean to teach us that. There is a place for food and sleep but we have not learned to enjoy that rightly until we have also learned that, if necessary, God can strengthen us even without them.

Beloved, is not our trouble this, that in the hour of testing we are more anxious to be delivered than to meet God's thought and glorify God's grace? What Christ was concerned for in that conflict was not so much to get bread as to show the all-sufficiency of God and stand obedient to His Father's will, trusting implicitly His Father's love.

Our blessed Lord has taught us this deep spiritual truth in one of His most profound discourses and left for our guidance through the Christian age the great principle on which He Himself built His own life and overcame the assault of the enemy in His body. That discourse was so marked in its teachings, so deep and heart-searching in its scope that most of His disciples were unable to accept it and, indeed, with the exception of the Twelve the whole of His Galilean flock grew tired of such deep teaching and utterly deserted Him on account of it. "This is a hard teaching," they replied. "Who can accept it?" (John 6:60).

That sermon was the wonderful discourse given about the living Bread in the sixth chapter of the Gospel of John. The one thought that pervades it is that we are to draw our lives both spiritually and physically directly from the Lord Jesus even as He draws His strength from the Father. Its one keynote is the profound verse, "Just as the living Father sent me and I live because of the

Father, so the one who feeds on me will live because of me" (6:57).

By eating Him, He explains explicitly that He means taking His flesh and blood as the source of life and strength. He tells us that this will give us an eternal life, life that will flow on even until the resurrection, for He adds in connection with it, that He will raise us up at the last day. As the babe lives upon its mother's life, the believer lives on Jesus' and the profound words become more true than any language can express, "in him we live and move and have our being" (Acts 17:28).

But this profound truth receives its deepest, largest unfolding in the later teachings of the Holy Spirit through the ministry and example of the Apostle Paul. It runs like a golden principle from the heavenly fountain through all his teachings and experience.

The Lord for the Body

With great vividness Paul unfolds the doctrine of our union with Jesus Christ, our living Head. "We are members," he says, "of his body" (Ephesians 5:30)—of His flesh and bones. The Lord is for our body and the body is for the Lord. Our bodies are the members of Christ and the temples of the Holy Spirit. The Spirit that dwells within us "give[s] life to [our] mortal bodies" (Romans 8:11). This certainly cannot mean our future body as it shall be raised from the tomb. It is the "death-doomed" body, as Rotherham happily translates it—the body in which the Spirit is now dwelling, liable to death, but not yet dead; and divinely equipped, exhilarated, renewed by the indwelling life of the Holy Spirit.

In the fourth chapter of Second Corinthians he unfolds this doctrine of the supernatural body more fully than anywhere else. There he tells us that his natural life is constantly exposed to death "so that the life of Jesus may also be revealed" in his mortal flesh (4:10).

This life of Jesus is something more distinct from and far transcending his own natural life. When they dragged him through the streets of Lystra and hurled him on the pavements as one dead the life of Paul was about gone, but it was then that the "life of Jesus" came to his relief and as the disciples stood around him in prayer and his own sinking heart was lifted up to heaven, there came a touch of divine quickening and he rose upon his feet and went forth again to his work on the borrowed strength of heaven.

So he went through life, not strong in himself, but saying that "we have this treasure in jars of clay to show that this all-surpassing power is from God and not from us" (4:7). And so, quoting from the fine translation of Rotherham, he adds, "On every side we are pressed hard but not hemmed in; without a way but not without a byway; pursued but not abandoned; thrown down but not destroyed, at all times the putting to death of Jesus in the body bearing about; that the life also of Jesus in our body might be made manifest" (4:8-10).

Space and time will not permit us to follow at greater length this sublime thought. We will only add one other illustration of it in his reference to the thorn in the flesh which is perplexing so many inquirers and expounders.

Now the principle we have been unfolding supplies the very solution of this difficult case. Supposing for the time that Paul's thorn was not literally removed in answer to his prayer, still the fact would remain that something was given to Paul in exchange which was better for him than if it had been removed, something in kind which really supplied the place of its removal. He calls it the power of Christ. It was not the comfort and consolation of Christ's love. It was not patience to bear it, but it was actually power through which he was enabled to do more than if the thorn had been taken away, so that he could say a little later, "The things that mark an apostle—signs, wonders and miracles—were done among you with great perseverance" (12:12). He actually affirmed while this thorn was still remaining, "when I am weak, then I am strong" (12:10).

Assuming then that it was a physical infirmity and that it was not taken away, yet it was perfectly certain that something was given to him that constituted real strength, ample strength, superior strength to even his own perfect soundness and health.

This is the very thing of which we have been speaking. It was an invisible life. It was a supernatural source of vitality. It was not a bigger wire, but a stronger current through the wire. It was the life of Jesus instead of the life of Paul.

Inner, Not Outer, Strength

This will explain many a perplexing experience with divine healing. Your actual physical condition is not always taken away, but if you would only keep looking to Jesus you would find an inner strength given to you, a supernatural spring in the depths of your being, a vigor and vitality that made you superior to the drain upon you of that depressing symptom and that carried you in spite of it with winged feet through all the pressures of your physical life.

God is thus trying to teach us to live in the unseen realm, to walk upon the waters of the spiritual sphere, to tread the seeming void by faith and find a rock beneath.

And so he sums up his sublime argument for the supernatural body in the fourth chapter of Second Corinthians by that passage which apart from this principle would be obscure: "Therefore we do not lose heart. Though outwardly we are wasting away, yet inwardly we are being renewed day by day" (4:16). As this whole discussion is about the physical life he must mean that the natural and material sources of our spiritual strength are failing, but the hidden and divine source within our being is renewed and strengthened. But he tells us that this is only while we look not at the things which are seen but at the things which are not seen. It is only while we dwell on the experience of faith in the immaterial realm, in the unseen region where God lives and we live with Him, having food to eat that the world knows nothing about (John 4:32), appropriating our very life from the heart of the risen Son of God.

In conclusion this great truth of the supernatural body is an intensely practical and present truth for answering unbelief. It is an answer to the unbelief of the age. Professor Tyndale challenged the disciples of Christ to produce an actual physical miracle. No wise man was rash enough to take up that challenge so presumptuously made, but God took it up. From that day there have been literally thousands of cases of divine healing as remarkable in many respects as those of the apostolic records.

God wants us today to show the unbelieving world that His presence and power are real on every plane of human life and experience, and although He will not give us signs when we tempt Him by asking for them, yet He will make us signs to the unbelieving world and confirm His Word with signs following if we are faithful to the testimony and claim by faith the fulfillment of His own promise.

Spiritual and Physical Intertwined

The experience of a supernatural body is a blessed auxiliary to the deeper life of the soul. The body is a conducting or a non-conducting medium of the Holy Spirit in His communications to the spirit, according as it is in harmony with God or out of actual touch with Him. Someone has used the phrase "a converted body." There are bodies that are divinely touched and there are others that are as cold and gross as the clods of clay beneath our feet. When God has to pass through the medium of a course physical organism to get into the heart there is obviously a distinct hindrance. There is a great difference between taking your dinner on a hot plate or a cold plate; a cold plate chills the best dinner ever served. And so the Holy Spirit wants the medium through which He ministers to our spirit to be itself spiritual. When our whole physical being is permeated with the presence of God and the baptism of the Holy Spirit, we are in more distinct touch with God's thoughts, influence and suggestions. Our very environment is holy and heavenly and the walls of the city are protected from the incursions of the enemy as well as the citadel itself.

Merely natural health and material and organs have about them an inborn tendency to selfish and even sensual gratification, but when Christ fills our hearts the very desire for unholy things is removed and we are saved from innumerable suggestions of evil that spring from the strong sensuous life of those who have never felt the touch of God in their mortal frame.

Divine healing in its deepest and highest sense saves from a thousand liabilities to self-indulgence and earthliness of thought, feeling and act. Our whole being becomes a well-tuned instrument on which God can play, and we learn to glorify Him in our body which is His, while the spirit sympathizes with the divine touch in all the lower realms of nature and every avenue of our being is thrown open to the unfolding presence of God, so that we cannot tell where the body ends and the spirit begins, but "HOLY TO THE LORD" (Exodus 28:36, Zechariah 14:20) is written on every fiber of our being.

Preparation for Service

The experience of this supernatural life greatly enhances our efficiency for service. Not only does it save us from innumerable physical hindrances and sources of selfish misery, murmuring and depression, not merely does it give us increased vigor and ability for arduous service and long endurance, but the quality of the service given by a body that is divinely touched is much higher. The voice that speaks and sings for God has more power in its tone and ministers grace more directly than if we were merely using an instrument of clay. The feet that are divinely touched not only go faster to bear the messages of God, but they accomplish more directly spiritual results. The grip of the hand is different. The grip of the hand communicates something which could never be expressed without this added touch of heaven.

It is not only the divine message and a divine

messenger but the very medium through which it goes has been spiritualized and made sacred by being itself steeped in the fountains of heavenly life and power.

Finally the Church of God needs especially today a new touch of supernatural power in the confirmation of her testimony to the world and especially to the heathen world.

While, as we have said in a former chapter, this truth is liable to extravagance, yet there is even a greater danger of overlooking it and sinking to the low plane of naturalism and rationalism in giving our testimony to mankind. In every age it ought still to be true: "God also testified to [the gospel] by signs, wonders and various miracles, and gifts of the Holy Spirit distributed according to his will" (Hebrews 2:4). If the Christ of Christianity is "the same yesterday and today and forever" (13:8), the Christianity of Christ ought also to be the same yesterday, today and forever.

CHAPTER 6

The Supernatural Hope

While we wait for the blessed hope—the glorious appearing of our great God and Savior, Jesus Christ. (Titus 2:13)

As you look forward to the day of God and speed its coming. (2 Peter 3:12)

In the opening verses of the chapter in Second Peter from which the last of these two texts is taken, the apostle speaks of a school of thinkers who would arise in the last days and should say, "Where is this 'coming' he promised? Ever since our fathers died, everything goes on as it has since the beginning of creation" (2 Peter 3:4). This is but another form of expressing the very doctrine which a certain school of philosophers and scientists are promulgating in this very day.

It is substantially the principle of the doctrine of evolution. Its vital principle is this: the things that are have been evolved out of similar things in the past and they will go on developing into similar unfoldings in the future. There has been no real crisis suspending the natural order of things and there will be none. Therefore, such a harsh, strained doctrine as that of the interposition of the supreme Being directly in the future history of this planet, and His advent on the stage of earth in personal form, does violence to all the finest instincts of culture and all the established principles of science.

It is the devil's own trick of trying to reduce everything in the universe to a rational basis and eliminate the supernatural not only from the past but from the future history of the human race, and making man and nature all sufficient and all in all.

Now, nature itself bears witness against this false assumption. The profoundest scientists themselves tell us that this world carries within its bosom the elements of destruction, and that in the very nature of things there are causes at work leading up to a great final catastrophe in the very orbits of the heavenly bodies. Humboldt himself, the prince of scientists, predicted a great terrestrial collapse at some future period in the lapse of ages. As Peter tells us in this passage, even the recent past of our planet's history bears witness to a tremendous convulsion when the flood of waters swept the whole human race away, foreshadowing the greater fact yet to come, when the flood of flame will wrap the world in final conflagration. The story of the past has not been evolution but revolution and a still greater catastrophe looms before us in the vision both of nature and of prophecy.

Then besides, the whole framework of our human life bears witness that the present is but an imperfect foreshadowing of something greater and more abiding. All we feel and see and know today is but the embryo of a boundless future. The deepest instincts of our nature tell us of a larger sphere, a loftier life and a more abiding home. Here we have scarcely learned to love when the grave closes over the objects of our affections. Our plans are only made when the rude hand of death or change dissolves the vision and defeats the project. Life is full of broken columns and new-made graves. The very creation groans for some better day and some great Deliverer. Every voice within us seems to cry,

> Beyond the flight of time,
>   Beyond the reign of death,
> There surely is some brighter clime
>   Where life is not a breath,
> Nor life's affections transient fires
> Whose spark flies upward and expires.
>
> There is a world above
>   Where parting is unknown,
> A long eternity of love
>   Formed for the good alone;
> And faith beholds our lost one's here
> Translated to that glorious sphere.

Thank God the light of revelation is clear and cloudless respecting this blessed hope. Undimmed and increasing it shines from the dawn of revelation to the glorious consummation.

Biblical Figures

Away back at the gate of Eden the mystic figure of the cherubim was a type of redeemed humanity, first in its glorious Head and ultimately in all its members. The face of the lion spoke of its kingliness; the face of the ox its strength; the face of the man its perfect humanness; the face of the soaring eagle its loftiness and union with the divine. All this was to be accomplished first in Christ and then in His redeemed ones. It was like a photograph placed at the gate of Eden showing the future glory of his race to poor broken-hearted Adam as he went forth a fugitive from the paradise that he had lost.

That is the vision God gives to every man who will accept restoration through the Lord Jesus Christ. Lost and sinful we may be, but someday we will be as glorious as our exalted Head.

Next we see this blessed hope as the theme which Enoch first preached and afterward exemplified. He was the first prophet of the second coming and when his ministry was finished God bore witness to it by taking him away to realize in his own person the glorious hope to which he had testified.

Noah and the deluge through which he passed set forth in figure some of the greatest truths

THE SUPERNATURAL HOPE 79

connected with the Lord's coming. While Enoch represented the translated saints who will be caught up before the storm, Noah represented rather the people of Israel who will pass through the tribulation and come out, as he did, on the other side to inherit the new earth. The times of Noah were typical of the times of the Son of Man, and the whole story of his supernatural deliverance foreshadows the closing days of the Christian age.

Abraham in like manner lived under the power of this coming age. While he received the land of promise in covenant yet he himself was a stranger in it and he died in faith of an inheritance which he should afterwards receive. The very reason why he so sacredly cherished the only spot on the ground he owned in Canaan, the cave of Machpelah, was because it was the burial place of his beloved wife and the pledge of God's covenant of the future inheritance of the land in the glorious resurrection. God's promise to him was for a thousand generations and it is not hard to conclude that those promises must yet be far in the future in their ultimate complete fulfillment.

In like manner Joseph showed his faith in the supernatural hope by giving commandment concerning his bones when dying. He wanted his very dust to have a part in the future inheritance of the land when he, with the saints of Israel, should stand in his lot at the end of days.

Time would fail to trace this hope through the psalms of David and the history of the Old Testament prophets. Suffice it to say that as the old dispensation came to its close amid the wreck of Israel and the utter failure of humanity to accomplish God's purpose, the light of the better hope began to shine amid the gathering darkness. Isaiah, Ezekiel, Jeremiah, Zechariah and, above all, Daniel looked out upon the distant future and saw and told the wondrous panorama of the ages and the glorious coming of Christ which was to be the consummation. Like the New Testament the Old closes with a grand apocalypse of the future.

The Life of Christ

The ministry of the Lord Jesus Christ was crowned at its highest point with a sublime object lesson of His own future advent. At the very time when He was turning from His marvelous work in Galilee, He took His disciples with Him to the heights of Hermon and for one bright lustrous hour He let the veil fall from the face of His deity and shed forth in all its effulgence His advent glory. In His own transfigured face and form they saw Him as He will come again, while in Moses and Elijah they had the vision, first of the sleeping dead as they will be raised and then of the living as they will be translated. All this, Peter tells us, was a vision of the power and coming of the Lord Jesus intended to cheer his heart and comfort others in view of the dark tribulations which were just before them.

In His last discourse, however, He formulated

the message of His coming with great fullness and, as He sat upon the side of Olivet the last week of His earthly life, He delivered with great definiteness and vividness the successive events of the Christian age and especially of its closing chapter. These wonderful discourses contain the substance of all later prophecies respecting the advent and are worthy of the profoundest study.

But after Pentecost the Holy Spirit unfolded this great truth with greater fullness. All the apostles are witnesses to it. Even on the day of Pentecost they clearly pointed out the connection between the Holy Spirit and the coming of the Lord. The two last promises of Jesus as He went away were the baptism of the Spirit and His own literal return. One of Peter's early sermons referred with great definiteness first to the "times of refreshing" (Acts 3:19) which the Spirit was to bring from the presence of the Lord, and then to the "time . . . to restore" (3:21) which the Lord Himself was to bring when the heavens which had received Him would give Him up for His final advent.

Paul wrote two of his epistles, the letters to the Thessalonians, with special reference to this great truth and again and again refers to it in all his letters as his own blessed inspiration and expectation.

Paul tells much of the "blessed hope" (Titus 2:13) and James, the most practical of them all and furthest removed from mysticism or dreaming of any sort, tells the struggling and oppressed

Christian of his day to leave their wrongs to be adjusted, not by trade unions and labor strikes, but by the coming of the Lord. And John, nearest to the Master's heart, and latest to give out His last messages, closes the sacred canon and seals the book of inspiration with the sublime Apocalypse which is one long bright vision of the Lord's coming and the events which precede and follow it.

The order of the New Testament is similar to the Old in its general scope and structure. There is first the narrative of facts; second, the teaching of the deeper spiritual truth; third, the prophetic revelation of the Father. God cannot trust us with the glorious doctrine of His coming until we are first established in the facts of Christianity and in the depths of the Spirit. Above all doctrines it is the least fitted to play with, to talk about, to lightly hold as a theory. We need to be deeply rooted and grounded in Christ before we can wisely grasp it or give it forth. But after we have received the Spirit in His fullness, one of His special ministries is to show us things to come, to open the gates of vision and unfold the prophetic Word.

The Visible Appearing of Christ

Now, as the Holy Spirit has revealed this glorious hope, its supernatural character will appear in several particulars.

First, it will bring a supernatural revelation of Christ. If we accept the fact that the Lord Jesus once resided upon this earth as a supernatural Man, why should it be thought strange that He should revisit it and dwell upon it for a longer time as its sovereign Lord? Christians of every name believe that the divine Person that once walked upon this earthly scene is residing somewhere now in the heavens in His actual and visible personality. It would be but a slight transition for Him to return in person to the world where He once dwelled. This is the common sense of the doctrine of the Lord's coming. "This same Jesus, who has been taken from you into heaven, will come back in the same way you have seen him go into heaven" (Acts 1:11). Of course, His coming will be different in this respect, that the veil of humiliation which obscured His deity during His earthly ministry will be forever dropped and He will shine forth in all the majesty of His deity and His universal lordship.

That this must mean a literal and visible appearing should scarcely need to be demonstrated. The strange theory of later centuries, which has been accepted by so large a portion of the Christian Church, has practically explained away the force and meaning of this blessed hope. According to this spiritualizing interpretation, the promise of His coming is substantially fulfilled in His personal indwelling in the hearts of His people and the triumph of the truths and principles of the gospel among all nations.

Now, in reply to the first, it is enough to say that the New Testament apostles enjoyed the indwelling of Christ as fully as any human being may expect to during the Christian age, and yet they constantly looked forward to an actual coming of Christ as the supreme object of their hope.

In respect to the other, it ought to be conclusive to remember that uniformly in speaking of Christ's coming the Holy Spirit represents the world at the time of His appearing as in no sense under the influence of the truth of the Spirit of God but really at the lowest ebb of sin and spiritual declension. If the Lord's coming is really the triumph of the truth, what can we make of such passages as these?

> When the Son of Man comes, will he find faith on the earth? (Luke 18:8)

> As it was in the days of Noah, so it will be at the coming of the Son of Man. (Matthew 24:37)

So far from the horoscope of prophecy revealing a future of Christian progress and worldwide righteousness under the present dispensation, the prophetic vision portrays an age of increasing unbelief, worldliness and sin growing more aggravated toward the close, while the true church of Christ as a little flock stands in the midst of prevailing declension, witnessing for Christ and waiting for His appearing. That appearing is always represented as a clearly marked and unmistakable event, as manifest and as transcendent as the lightning which shines from one end of heaven to the other. It is a great supernatural fact and the central figure of it will be the person of Christ Himself revealed in all His glory not only before the admiring eyes of His saints but before the vision of a startled world.

Transformation of Believers

Second, the believers will be supernaturally transformed. This blessed hope is going to bring not only the glorified Christ but the glorification of His saints. Those who sleep will be raised from the dead by a supernatural and instantaneous manifestation of the almighty power of Christ, and the living will be changed immediately afterwards. The change which will come to both will bring a complete transformation into the perfect likeness of their glorified Head.

The event is described in the most transcendent language. He "who, by the power that enables him to bring everything under his control, will transform our lowly bodies so that they will be like his glorious body" (Philippians 3:21).

In his argument from analogy in the 15th chapter of First Corinthians, the Apostle Paul gives us some hints of the transcending glory of the resurrection body. He tells us it will be a spiritual body and a celestial body. It will be substantially the same as the body that sank to the tomb and yet it will be unspeakably different. The resemblance will be similar to that of the bare grain which we plant in the soil to the beautiful plant which springs from it covered with blossom and abundant fruit. As the orange tree with its fresh and fragrant blossoms and its golden hanging fruit is to a little dry orange seed planted in the soil, so will the body of the glory be to this corruptible form which we lay down at death. "It is sown in dishonor, it is raised in glory; it is sown in weakness, it is raised in power; it is sown a natural body, it is raised a spiritual body" (15:43-44).

The blessed truth of the resurrection and the glorified body is beyond the search of human philosophy and science. It is not a truth that can be learned by the ordinary processes of human knowledge. It is distinctly supernatural, and it must be accepted by faith as a doctrine of divine revelation.

And yet, even nature has some beautiful parables of it. The process of germination from the buried seed is a divine type of the resurrection. The exquisite silver jewel, which the chemist can dissolve in acid until it disappears from view and then by precipitating some new acid into the solution can bring it back again and cast it into the crucible, remaking it in some more beautiful form, is another prototype.

This is man's rude anticipation of God's glorious supernatural redemption. The supreme illustration and confirmation of this stupendous truth must ever be the simple fact that Christ Himself, the Head of humanity, has died and risen from the dead, and His glorified body is the pattern and guarantee of our resurrection.

Amazing Changes in Nature

Third, the material world will have a supernatural transformation. Not only will man be changed, but his home will be the subject of a transformation quite as wonderful. The traces of sin and the memories of suffering and death will be obliterated. The cemeteries will disappear. The awful fact of death will be but a memory of the distant past and the cemeteries will not only give up their dead but will cease to separate and destroy. The wild and savage instincts of the lower orders of creation will be subjected; the lion will become gentle as the ox; the wolf will lie down with the lamb; the asp and scorpion will cease to sting; the feebler orders of the natural creation will no longer groan under the law that makes them a prey to the stronger.

The very law of gravitation will be changed and in the New Jerusalem the streets will be vertical as well as horizontal and we will pass up and down as freely as we pass to and fro, for earth's attraction will be forever broken and the center of gravitation will be the Lord Himself. The barren desert will "blossom as the rose" (Isaiah 35:1, KJV). Earth's climates will be changed and "The sun will not beat upon them, nor any scorching heat" (Revelation 7:16), nor will the biting frosts and winters distress again in the new earth's summerland of love. Earth will be a heaven below. Paradise will be restored. The curse will be canceled and all that infinite wisdom, love and power can do to make this planet the paragon of nature will crown the glorious work of complete redemption.

A Change in Government

Fourth, this blessed hope will bring a supernatural transformation in the providence of God and the government of the world and the universe. Man's government has been proved and tried and found a pitiful failure.

In the vision of Daniel the kings of earth are represented as a destructive power of so many wild beasts, but the glorious promise is given that the saints of the most High will at length take the kingdom: "Then the sovereignty, power and greatness of the kingdoms under the whole heaven will be handed over to the saints, the people of the Most High. His kingdom will be an everlasting kingdom, and all rulers will worship and obey him" (Daniel 7:27). Christ Himself will be the sovereign Ruler of the world. Zechariah has told us in the most definite language, "The LORD will be king over the whole earth. On that day there will be one LORD, and his name the only name. . . . Then the survivors from all the nations that have attacked Jerusalem will go up year after year to worship the King, the LORD Almighty, and to celebrate the Feast of Tabernacles" (Zechariah 14:9, 16).

This is the very song of the redeemed saints: "You have made them to be a kingdom and priests to serve our God, and they will reign on the earth" (Revelation 5:10).

The very promise of the closing vision of the Apocalypse is, "Blessed and holy are those who have part in the first resurrection. The second death has no power over them, but they will be priests of God and of Christ and will reign with him for a thousand years" (20:6).

Among earth's vast burdens has been the curse of corrupt government; her political and social systems will never be right until He will come whose right it is to reign. Christ's coming is the only remedy for the wrongs of society and the disease of the body politic. Let us be true to the responsibility of Christian citizenship but let us ever remember that our citizenship is in heaven whence we are expecting earth's true King.

The new adjustment of this earth will affect all other worlds. There is a sense in which Christ's redemption is to reconcile all things both in heaven and on earth. Just what all this will mean is impossible even in the light of Scripture to foretell fully, but beyond the millennial years there will certainly be a larger and grander unfolding in the ages of ages resulting at length in the new heavens and new earth, wherein righteousness alone will dwell and the application in some way of the great principle unfolded and established in the story of human redemption to all the distant worlds of space and all parts of God's universal empire. Perhaps these constellations are yet to be distant colonies from this redeemed planet, and the vast dominions and principalities over which the saints will reign as the promised reward of their service and fidelity here.

The forms of human life during these coming ages are sufficiently outlined to make this at least clear: during the millennial age there will be three distinct peoples upon this planet. First will be the nations of earth which will still exist on the human plane as they do today, excepting only that they will be the subjects of Christ's kingdom and enjoy the blessed privileges of His universal reign of righteousness and peace.

The next will be the Jewish nation which is to continue in fulfillment of the promise to Abraham and David for a thousand generations. This will be the supreme nation, and Israel from Jerusalem will exercise a worldwide influence of a sovereign city, governed directly by God Himself and fulfilling the high conception of ancient theocracy without its imperfections and mournful failure. David is to reign over his ancient kingdom as the direct vice-regent of Christ, and Abraham is to enjoy with all his seed the glorious fulfillment of the mighty promises for which he has waited so long, and Israel is to realize literally as a nation the yet-unfulfilled vision of ancient Hebrew prophecy.

But there will be a third race, namely, the risen and translated saints who will reign upon the earth and yet possess a heavenly life and a spiritual body. Their government of the world will be under the immediate direction of the Lord Jesus Christ Himself, their ever-present King.

They will be the executive officers of this kingdom and their power may be similar to that of angelic beings, who now have so prominent a part in the affairs of nature and are employed by God in controlling the affairs of nations and checking and counteracting in human affairs the hate of Satan and the objections and oppositions of wicked men.

The risen saints in the millennial age will have free and constant access to the material world and the whole system of human life, visiting men and often engaging in conflicts with them, but living on a far higher plane. Like the angels who came to Abraham and like the Lord Himself during the 40 days, they will doubtless be able to eat and drink and sit down in simple loving fellowship at human tables and in earth's family circles, but they will not need the nourishment of food, refreshment of sleep or the supply of present physical wants. Their life will be supernatural and directly sustained from the Lord Himself. As Christ has told us, they will be in some sense like the angels who "neither marry nor [are] given in marriage" (Matthew 22:30), neither can they die anymore, being the children of the resurrection. It may be that we will dwell with our glorified Lord not exactly on earth but perhaps above it in the New Jerusalem, which may be the dwelling place of the saints during the millennial age as well as afterwards, a city let down from heaven, yet touching earth and in constant intercourse with its inhabitants.

Blessings of This Hope

We need, of course, to be careful of ideal or daring speculations respecting things which so far transcend our present range of thought and conception, and yet we know enough of our Lord's resurrection life during the 40 days to inspire our hearts with the most delightful anticipations of the glorified life that awaits us so soon, and of which He has said to us respecting many a fond hope which perhaps we could not prove and yet which we dare to cherish, "If it were not so, I would have told you" (John 14:2).

Antidote to Humanism

In conclusion, the supernatural hope of the Lord's coming is a present truth because, in the first place, it is a true antidote to the humanism of our age. Self-sufficient man is building his tower of Babel and projecting his future utopias of ambition and imagination. But over all these God is laughing from the heavens and saying, "I have installed my King on Zion, my holy hill" (Psalm 2:6). Let men dream their fond and foolish dreams. Let them make their investments and calculations for centuries to come, but we look for "the city with foundations, whose architect and builder is God" (Hebrews 11:10).

Explanation of History

Second, this blessed hope is the only explanation and key for facts of human history and providences and the problems and perplexities which they create. All the past becomes plain if we read it in the light of God's plan, and contemporary history is reduced to simplicity as we see in the center of all the movements of our time God's distinct purpose to prove earthly governments a failure, to overrule the affairs of states and nations for the calling out of His people from all lands, to preserve the seed of Abraham distinct from and supremely above all other races, and to put down the systems of iniquity which are hindering His purposes concerning Israel and the Church. Read in the light of prophecy, the rise and fall of Babylon, Persia, Greece and Rome can be understood; we can understand the broken maps of Europe and the dismembered kingdoms of the past; we can understand the rise and decadence of Papal and Muslim powers; we can understand the supremacy of the English people; we can understand the growing strength of Russia in the north; we can understand the Turkish massacres, the Armenian horrors, the outbursts of Muslim fanaticism, the persecution of Israel, and enjoy the remarkable rallying of the nation around the standard of Zion and the hope of a speedy restoration of their national existence. We can understand the increasing commercial activity and strange wickedness of our age. We can see the deeper life of the little flock and the broader enterprise of worldwide missions. He that is Head over all things for His body, the Church, is preparing the last great conflict and marshaling the forces of earth and heaven for the day of the Lord.

Our Highest Inspiration

Again, this supernatural hope is the highest inspiration of Christian life and work. There is no truth more inspiring, calling us out from this doomed earth to fix our hopes and ambitions in the coming kingdom. There is no truth more sanctifying, impelling us to make sure not only of the white robe of holiness, but the wedding robe of the deeper love that alone can fit us for the meeting with our Bridegroom, and calling us to receive the baptism of the Holy Spirit as the oil in our vessels which will save us from the folly and failure of the foolish virgins.

Incentive to Service

In like manner, it is the great incentive to diligent and faithful service. We are working intelligently with a well-defined aim and a glorious expectation. We are not beating air and looking in vain for the conversion of the world, but we are cooperating with our coming Lord and giving the gospel as a witness to all nations as the one last condition preceding His advent. Christians are the men most intensely aroused to the necessity and importance of this great work because they understand the times and know what Israel ought to do, and are giving out in the last two movements of our age the message to the streets and lanes of the city, and the message to the highways and hedges and the outcast millions of the world.

A Convicting Message

And we believe that this blessed supernatural hope constitutes the most convincing and convicting message to lost men, and especially to the unevangelized nations of our time. There seems to be some special emphasis in the phrase, "gospel of the kingdom" (Matthew 24:14), used in connection with witnessing unto all nations before the end comes.

It seems to be suggested at least that the messengers are to go forth with a specific warning of the immediate coming of the King. May it be that we have not used as definitely and emphatically as we might this great message of such world-awakening power.

We remember that when Jonah went to the Ninevites as an ambassador of heaven with a stormy announcement that within 40 days the King of kings would deal in judgment with one of the wicked nations of earth, the whole nation from the king to the lowest slave were moved to fear and repentance, and in sackcloth and ashes sat and obtained the mercy of Jehovah.

We know that when Paul preached to the Thessalonians this must have been his message to them, for he tells them in his first epistle that they turned from idols to serve the living and true God and wait for His Son in heaven.

We remember also that in the last missionary

picture of the Apocalypse, the angel who bears the everlasting gospel to all kindreds and nations and tribes and tongues (Revelation 14:6) proclaims to them that the hour of God's judgment has come and calls upon them with the stupendous call to meet their Judge. This is the present truth not only of the Church of God against the worldliness and skepticism of our Christian lands but especially the present truth which we are to go forth as ambassadors for Christ and deliver with divine authority and emphatic pointedness as His last message to the ungodly nations of the heathen world.

It is an encouraging fact that today the great majority of foreign missionaries at present on the field fully believe this truth. May the Lord give wisdom and power rightly to divide it and mightily to proclaim it to a careless world.

CHAPTER 7

The Supernatural Work

> *We are his workmanship, created in Christ Jesus unto good works, which God hath before ordained that we should walk in them. (Ephesians 2:10, KJV)*

The apostle here declares that our works are "prepared" (for that is the true translation of the word "ordained") "that we should walk in them." They are not our works, but His supplied to us through the Holy Spirit and the inworking of Christ, and we just work them out "with all his energy, which so powerfully works in [us]" (Colossians 1:29). Our whole life must be supernatural to the close, and our very service must be received before it can be performed—"receiving a kingdom that cannot be shaken, let us be thankful, and so worship God acceptably with reverence and awe" (Hebrews 12:28).

We must have supernatural power for our work. We must pass the sentence of death upon our natural enthusiasm, energy and zeal; and, dying to our own strength, we must receive power through the Holy Spirit and do our work in Him.

Moses had to be rejected when he stepped forth at the age of 40 in his own enthusiasm to deliver Israel. Afterwards, when he came back at 80, a broken man, humbled and conscious of his inefficiency, God could use him, like His own rod, an instrument in the hands of Jehovah.

Christ Himself continually recognized His power for service as divinely supplied. "By myself I can do nothing," He said; "I judge only as I hear" (John 5:30). "It is the Father, living in me, who is doing his work" (14:10). Therefore He did not begin His public ministry until He received the Holy Spirit and there was added to His divine Personality a second divine Personality—the third Person of the Godhead. And as He went through His earthly ministry there were two Persons united in His life work, the Son of God and the Spirit of God. He chose to be dependent upon the Spirit in order that He might be the more perfect type of us in our dependence.

Therefore His disciples were bidden to tarry in Jerusalem until they should be endued with power from on high. They were not permitted to go out in their own strength, but had to lean upon the Spirit for their wisdom, courage, faith and complete efficiency.

Wait for the Holy Spirit

No man is fitted for the humblest service in the

Church of God until he receives the divine baptism of the Holy Spirit. The mother needs it in the nursery, the Sunday school teacher in his class, the preacher in his pulpit, the soul winner in his dealings with the inquirer and the saint in his ministry of prayer in the secret closet.

There is no truth that needs to be more emphasized in this age of smartness and human self-sufficiency than the imperative necessity of the baptism of the Holy Spirit as the condition of all effective Christian work. We must tarry before we go.

It pays to wait. A traveler pursued by his enemies lingered five minutes at the blacksmith's shop to have his horse reshod, and while some might have thought he was foolish thus to delay, yet he was truly wise, for as they drew near at the last moment and shouted their expected triumph he leaped into the saddle and was soon far in the distance. A week spent at the source of faith and power will bring more effective service than years of human effort in the energy of our highest gifts and loftiest genius.

We must have a supernatural plan. In the working out of a military campaign the commander relies upon the intelligent cooperation of his subordinate officers. If one division of the army were to rush into the attack heedless of the plan of the leader, it might hinder instead of help. A very small force judiciously used at the salient point of attack or defense often turns an enemy's flank and changes the issue of a decisive battle.

Christ has a plan in His mediatorial work. He does not send us forth to draw our bow at a venture and run wherever our fancy may dispose us, but He wants us to understand His method and work according to His great purpose. It is foreshadowed in the promise of the Spirit (Acts 1:8), the gospel for the center first, and then for the circumference, and then for the uttermost parts of the earth.

That plan was more fully unfolded at the first great council of the Christian Church in the 15th chapter of Acts and consists of three great sections: first, a visit to the Gentiles to take out of them a people for His name; second, the return of the Lord and the restoration of Israel; third, the millennial reign with the ingathering of all the Gentiles.

A wise worker will work according to this plan. He will not attempt today the ingathering of all the Gentiles, but will be occupied with the outgathering from them of the few who are to be the firstfruits for His coming. He will not be devoting his attention to Israel supremely, for the restoration of Israel is to come with the return of the Lord. His chief business will be to give the gospel to the Gentiles and gather out of them a people for His name.

This will save us many a bitter disappointment. We will not be found trying to convert all the people in the world and stop all the abuses of our time. This belongs to the next dispensation. Rather, we are to be busily occupied in the great missionary work of the age and the bringing back of our King.

Wait for God's Directing

We must have supernatural direction. It is possible to have a divine plan and yet run at our own impulse in the direction of our work. This was Saul's mistake. God sent him as Israel's king to destroy His enemies, but Saul took the reins into his own hand and, instead of waiting for Samuel to lead, stepped out in front, and by his presumption destroyed himself and his kingdom.

This was Joshua's danger. God had sent him and promised to bless him in bringing Israel into the Land of Promise. Joshua had an idea that he was to lead the armies of Israel, and so God had to meet him with a drawn sword and lay him on his face at the very outset of his career, and remind him that He, not Joshua, was Captain of the Lord's host. Then Joshua became conqueror when he simply followed his conquering Leader.

Very early in the Acts of the Apostles Philip had to learn this lesson. Preaching in Samaria with wonderful success, it seemed on all human principles that this was his immediate duty. But suddenly the Spirit commanded him to go down into the desert, and he was wise and faithful enough to obey, to leave his work in Samaria and to go down 100 miles into the lone wilderness until at last the leading was made plain, and the prince of Ethiopia was converted to God and became the pioneer of the gospel in the great continent of Africa.

Even Paul and Silas had to be severely taught that they must go every moment at the direction of their supernatural Leader. Rushing forward in the accomplishment of their plans into Bithynia, Mysia and Asia, they were suddenly stopped by the Holy Spirit: "the Spirit of Jesus would not allow them to" (Acts 16:7). They had gone beyond their personal Leader, and they were compelled to retrace their steps and get still before God and wait for new orders. They seemed to be doing good, but God was not pleased and would not have it.

He does not even want good work if it is not His very work for us at that very time. It is not true to say, "I am doing some good; I am doing the best I know how." True service is doing the very thing that God has for us, doing it in His strength and wholly pleasing Him. If we are not doing this we may be hindering Him by our very Christian work. It is a serious question whether much of the religious work today is not entirely out of God's will. I believe that many a man that is preaching today in an American pulpit ought to be in some foreign field, and because he is not in God's will he blights his blessings and lets his church run into foolishness, worldliness and sometimes infidelity.

So Paul called a halt and waited for his Leader to point the way, and then he found that way led them out of the field that He was cultivating across the Aegean Sea into the continent of Europe and the kingdom of Greece.

God had a great ultimate purpose in that which Paul could not foresee. He knew that the nations of modern history were to have their theater of action in that great continent. There our forefathers were to be born and thence were we to spring, and well may we thank God that Paul obeyed that divine leading and gave up his own work to the work of the Master.

Beloved, are you doing the very work God has for you? Did He redeem you for the purpose of spending your life in selfish amusement, or even in half-hearted conventional formalism which you call Christian work? Go to your knees and find out whether you are going to discover too late that you have lost your way and have spent your strength in vain.

God Gives the Increase

Last, we need supernatural efficiency. God must give the increase and bring the fruition as well as lead the way, and He does give efficiency for the humblest ministries which are performed in Him. The seed may have seemed to lie in silence, but it is sure to spring forth and bring the harvest.

A single sentence spoken by Charles Spurgeon in an empty hall that the carpenters were fixing for his next Sabbath's service reached the ear of a mechanic at his workbench in an adjoining shop. Twenty-five years later Spurgeon found, when that man was on his deathbed, that he had been saved through that arrow shot at a venture because it was in the Holy Spirit.

A little English girl lived and died unknown to all but her family and her pastor, but the beautiful story of her life was written by her minister, Leigh Richmond, in a tract called *The Dairyman's Daughter*. That little tract fell into the hands of a young English noble who was wasting his splendid intellect in dissipation, and William Wilberforce arose from his perusal a consecrated Christian and became the emancipator of all the slaves in the British Empire. William Wilberforce wrote a little book called *The Practical View of Religion*, and it fell into the hands of an easygoing Scottish preacher who was actually thinking of giving up his pulpit to teach mathematics, but out of that little book was born the mighty soul of Thomas Chalmers, and out of his life came the Scottish Disruption, the Free Church and the great movement for Christ and mission which that noble church has led and to which many of us owe our Christian hopes.

How marvelous the chain of divine working! How mighty the efficiency of a little word! How immortal the Word of God which lives and abides forever!

We will not always be conscious of the power. Indeed, it is our weakness that God most frequently uses. A little message spoken in great humility will become a seed in some other heart whose fruit will shake like Lebanon, and the blessing cover the earth and fill the heavens.

But God chose the foolish things of the world to shame the wise; God chose the weak things of the world to shame the strong. He chose the lowly things of this world and the despised things—and the things that are not—to nullify the things that are, so that no one may boast before him. It is because of him that you are in Christ Jesus, who has become for us wisdom from God—that is, our righteousness, holiness and redemption. Therefore, as it is written: "Let him who boasts boast in the Lord." (1 Corinthians 1:27-31)

What, after all, is Apollos? And what is Paul? Only servants, through whom you came to believe—as the Lord has assigned to each his task. I planted the seed, Apollos watered it, but God made it grow. So neither he who plants nor he who waters is anything, but only God, who makes things grow. . . . So then, no more boasting about men! All things are yours, whether Paul or Apollos or Cephas or the world or life or death or the present or the future—all are yours, and you are of Christ, and Christ is of God. (3:5-7, 21-23)

SCRIPTURE INDEX

Genesis
1:1 5
3:24 60
4:26 46
11:4 12-13
11:7 13
17:1 7

Exodus
3:12 9
3:14 8
28:36 73
33:15 9
33:17 9

Leviticus
19:18 40

Deuteronomy
8:3 62

Joshua
1:5 9
1:9 9
5:13 9
5:14 9
5:15 9
14:8 63
14:10 63
14:11 63

2 Chronicles
36:23 42-43

Job
38:7 36

Psalms
2:6 92
18:34 64
103:3 64
103:4 64
103:5 64
119:89 26

Song of Songs
8:5 50

Isaiah
25:9 15
35:1 87

Jeremiah
33:2 10
33:3 .... 10, 44

Ezekiel
36:27 38

Daniel
7:27 88

Haggai
1:2 12
2:5 11

Zechariah
14:9 88
14:16 88
14:20 73

Matthew
4:4 65
5:48 40
7:16 33-34
11:4 52
11:5 52
16:18 46
22:30 91
24:14 95
24:37 84
28:18 .... 12, 42, 53
28:20 .... 12, 42, 53

Luke
6:27 40
6:28 40
18:8 84

John
1:13 36
1:16 39
3:30 13
4:32 71
4:42 29
5:30 98
6:57 67
6:60 66
11:23 58
11:24 58
11:25 59
11:26 59
13:34 40
14:2 92
14:10 98
14:23 37
16:8 52
18:36 50
19:24 26
19:28 26
19:36 26
20:17 37

Acts
1:8 100
1:11 83
2:41 48
3:19 81
3:21 81
11:26 46
16:7 102
17:28 67

Romans
1:16 52
4:17 8

4:19 61
4:20 7-8
4:21 7-8
8:11 .... 57, 67
8:15 37
8:23 57
8:28 41
8:29 41

1 Corinthians
1:27 105
1:28 105
1:29 105
1:30 ....38-39, 105
1:31 ....38-39, 105
3:5 105
3:6 105
3:7 105
3:11 47
3:21 105
3:22 105
3:23 105
8:6 3
12:12 47
12:13 48-49
15:43 86
15:44 86

2 Corinthians
1:22 57
4:7 68
4:8 68-69

4:9 68-69
4:10 68-69
4:16 70
5:5 57
12:9 12
12:10 69
12:12 69

Galatians
2:20 33

Ephesians
1:14 57
2:10 97
5:25 45
5:26 45
5:27 .... 45, 53-54
5:30 67

Philippians
3:21 85
4:19 6

Colossians
1:29 97

Titus
2:13 .... 14, 75, 81

Hebrews
2:4 74
8:5 48

11:3 10
11:10 92
12:23 55
12:28 97
13:8 74

1 Peter

1:23 17
1:24 17
1:25 17

2 Peter

1:12 1
3:4 75
3:12 75

1 John

3:1 36
3:2 15

Revelation

3:2 50
5:10 88-89
7:16 87
12:1 53
14:6 96
20:6 89
21:9 54
22:13 5